The
Forgotten
Cross

*Some neglected aspects of
the cross of Christ*

Lee Gatiss

EP BOOKS
Faverdale North
Darlington
DL3 0PH, England

web: http://www.epbooks.org

e-mail: sales@epbooks.org

EP Books are distributed in the USA by:
JPL Distribution
3741 Linden Avenue Southeast
Grand Rapids, MI 49548
E-mail: orders@jpldistribution.com
Tel: 877.683.6935

British Library Cataloguing in Publication Data available

ISBN 978–1–78397–070–4

Endorsements

Here is a steady flow of down-to-earth insights into cross-shaped living. Thank you, Lee Gatiss, for your wisdom.

—*J. I. Packer, Board of Governors' Professor of Theology at Regent College in Vancouver*

This book of expositions by Lee Gatiss is an important reminder that, in our warranted zeal for the truth of penal substitution, we must not downplay or ignore the rich and full range of the achievements of the Cross, and its many applications to our lives. An important and edifying volume!

—*Tim Keller, Redeemer Presbyterian Church, New York City*

In the business of proclaiming the meaning of the cross there have been major battles to protect the key elements of the gospel of Christ crucified. Lee Gatiss is no stranger to the battle to maintain, for example, the significance of the cross as a penal sacrifice for sin. But sometimes the fog of war obscures other landmarks which tie the cross to the life of the church and the experience of the Christian. Without diminishing the major truths of the cross he skillfully unpacks the message of the cross for the church and the believer in the struggles of daily life. What he has written will warm the heart and strengthen the nerve of God's people as we join Christ 'outside the camp' where He was crucified and we will be encouraged to bear our own 'cross' as we follow after Him.

—Liam Goligher, Senior Minister, Tenth Presbyterian Church, Philadelphia

'Christ died for our sins according to the Scriptures' lies at the heart of the gospel. But what exactly are these sins (plural)? Not only many, surely, but diverse, subtle, deceitful, harmful. If so, Christ's death must be multivalent, deeper, richer, more adequate than merely a kind of mathematical exchange. If so, where do we begin? 'At Calvary's cross is where you begin.' And like John Bunyan's Evangelist, Lee Gatiss and his book *The Forgotten Cross* will be good and reliable guides to help us do just that. I hope this book will be a real beginning of a larger view of Christ and his work for many readers.

—Sinclair B. Ferguson, Senior Minister of the First Presbyterian Church in Columbia, South Carolina

Contents

Preface

The Heart of the Cross

The one thing I'm most passionate about as a Christian and as a minister is Christ. And right at the heart of what it means to know Christ is the cross—his death. That's what thrills me as a believer and as a pastor—God's love for us shown in the death of his Son in our place.

One of the first parts of the Bible I committed to memory as a Christian was Isaiah 53:5–6.

> He was pierced for our transgressions;
> he was crushed for our iniquities;
> upon him was the chastisement that brought us
>   peace,
> and with his wounds we are healed.
> All we like sheep have gone astray;
> we have turned—every one—to his own way;
> and the LORD has laid on him
> the iniquity of us all.

I remember how excited I was when I first saw the New Testament writers applying this Old Testament passage to Jesus, and realizing what it meant.

This vital and pivotal teaching of the Bible must lie at the heart of all we believe about Jesus and his death. 'Christ redeemed us from the curse of the law, by becoming a curse for us,' said the Apostle Paul (Galatians 3:13). Jesus took my place, and was cursed by God so that I will not be. Or as Peter says, 'Christ also suffered once for sins, the righteous for the unrighteous, that he might bring us to God' (1 Peter 3:18). 'In my place condemned he stood, sealed my pardon with his blood' as an old hymn puts it.[1]

Modern people, even many modern Christians, don't like to think of God as angry at sin. Talk of his 'wrath' scares or horrifies them, as if it were some primitive barbarism to be eradicated from our memory and replaced by something 'nicer'.[2] But as Leon Morris once wrote, 'Those who object to the conception of the wrath of God should realize that what is meant is not some irrational passion bursting forth uncontrollably, but a burning zeal for the right coupled with a perfect hatred for everything that is evil.'[3]

Surely we want a God who loves what is right and hates what is wrong? We don't want an apathetic God who just lets us get on with it, wrecking ourselves, each other, and his world in the process. But as Morris concludes, 'The Scripture is clear that the wrath of God is visited upon sinners or else the Son of God dies for them.'[4] Either we are punished, or someone takes our place. Either we die, or he dies, but the option of just forgetting about our sin is not a biblical one.

Some people have pejoratively called this 'cosmic child abuse'. They wince at the idea of singing 'on that cross, as Jesus died, the wrath of God was satisfied',[5] and they try instead to change the words to fit their own more liberal understanding. They are full of wrath against the idea of God's wrath, and the thought that Jesus has borne the full brunt of it for us.

As so often, John Stott put it brilliantly. He said, 'in and through the person of his Son, God himself bore the penalty which he himself inflicted.' The mysterious unity of the Father and the Son made it possible for God to both inflict punishment for sin and endure that same punishment for sin at the same time.[6]

This is not mechanistic or impersonal. As Garry Williams rightly says, 'in bearing the punishment of sin on the cross, the divine Word as a man endured the consequences of the personal confrontation between God and sinful men and women. The punishment involved the very being of God himself'.[7] Or as Jim Packer summed it up in his magnificent essay, *What did the cross achieve?* 'The penalty due to me for my sins, whatever it was, was paid for me by Jesus Christ, the Son of God, in his death on the cross.'[8]

This way of understanding the cross is sometimes called 'penal substitution'. That is, it is about punishment (the Latin for which is *poena*) being taken *in my place* (substitution). I want to affirm with all my heart that

God the Son's punishment-taking, in-my-place death is a magnificent centrepiece for all Christian theology. As I've read more and more church history over the years it has also become clear to me that this way of looking at things is not just something taught by the great evangelical scholars and preachers over the last century. As Steve Jeffery, Mike Ovey, and Andrew Sach have nicely demonstrated, 'the doctrine of penal substitution has been affirmed from the earliest days of the Christian church, and has continued to find a place in the mainstream of historic Christian theology throughout the last two thousand years.'[9]

Without penal substitution, I would be nowhere as a Christian. I wouldn't have a hope. So I'm passionate about it, and utterly committed to it theologically and pastorally. How else can I stand before a holy God on judgment day or come to him in prayer even, if I myself have to bear the punishment for my sins?

But the problem is, Morris, Stott, Packer, Williams, Jeffery, Ovey, Sach, and many others have done such a good job persuading many of us that this is a true and biblical perspective on the cross, that we might think we've got the atonement sussed now. We may delude ourselves that we know all about the cross. We're sorted on that.

But I wonder. I wonder, have we missed something in the midst of all the debates about penal substitution that have raged in recent years? Have we forgotten, perhaps, about other aspects of the death of Christ which the Bible also speaks of? Has fighting in one corner left us blind to some of the important things God has to say to us elsewhere in his word?

Well, the more I've delved into the Bible's teaching on the cross, the more I've been left with the feeling that there are indeed some forgotten or at least neglected dimensions to Christ's death that we would do well to recover.

That should *not* be taken as a criticism of the heroes and friends who have written so compellingly on penal substitution. It is simply to say that we haven't exhausted it yet. The cross demonstrates the *manifold* wisdom of God, and we can't say everything there is to say about it in one small book or even a whole shelf load.

The Bible explores and applies what Jesus did on the cross in a multitude of different ways. Penal substitution is one of them—indeed, it's the most important one, I think, because without it other ways of looking at the cross end up being inadequate for my salvation. But that's not to say that penal substitution alone is fully adequate to meet my needs.

Without penal substitution we don't understand the cross at all. But that's not to say it is comprehensive. On the cross, Christ exhausted the punishment due to sinners. But even if we know that, and revel in it, we have not exhausted the depths of glory in that spectacular act of sacrificial love.

On the cross, God did more than punish Jesus in our place. So much more. And that's what I want us to explore together in this short little book: *The forgotten cross*, some aspects of the death of Christ that are opened up for us in the Bible but which, with very good excuses perhaps, we may have neglected in evangelical circles of late.

1 Corinthians 1

The Cross and Success

*P*aul, called by the will of God to be an apostle of Christ Jesus, and our brother Sosthenes,

² *To the church of God that is in Corinth, to those sanctified in Christ Jesus, called to be saints together with all those who in every place call upon the name of our Lord Jesus Christ, both their Lord and ours:*

³ *Grace to you and peace from God our Father and the Lord Jesus Christ.*

⁴ *I give thanks to my God always for you because of the grace of God that was given you in Christ Jesus, ⁵ that in every way you were enriched in him in all speech and all knowledge—⁶ even as the testimony about Christ was confirmed among you—⁷ so that you are not lacking in any gift, as you wait for the revealing of our Lord Jesus Christ, ⁸ who will sustain you to the end, guiltless in the day of our Lord Jesus Christ. ⁹ God is faithful, by whom you were called into the fellowship of his Son, Jesus Christ our Lord.*

[10] *I appeal to you, brothers, by the name of our Lord Jesus Christ, that all of you agree, and that there be no divisions among you, but that you be united in the same mind and the same judgment.* [11] *For it has been reported to me by Chloe's people that there is quarrelling among you, my brothers.* [12] *What I mean is that each one of you says, 'I follow Paul,' or 'I follow Apollos,' or 'I follow Cephas,' or 'I follow Christ.'* [13] *Is Christ divided? Was Paul crucified for you? Or were you baptized in the name of Paul?* [14] *I thank God that I baptized none of you except Crispus and Gaius,* [15] *so that no one may say that you were baptized in my name.* [16] *(I did baptize also the household of Stephanas. Beyond that, I do not know whether I baptized anyone else.)* [17] *For Christ did not send me to baptize but to preach the gospel, and not with words of eloquent wisdom, lest the cross of Christ be emptied of its power.*

[18] *For the word of the cross is folly to those who are perishing, but to us who are being saved it is the power of God.* [19] *For it is written,*

'I will destroy the wisdom of the wise,

and the discernment of the discerning I will thwart.'

[20] *Where is the one who is wise? Where is the scribe? Where is the debater of this age? Has not God made foolish the wisdom of the world?* [21] *For since, in the wisdom of God, the world did not know God through wisdom, it pleased God through the folly of what we preach to save those who believe.* [22] *For Jews demand signs and Greeks seek wisdom,* [23] *but we preach Christ crucified, a stumbling block to Jews and folly to Gentiles,* [24] *but to those who are called, both Jews and Greeks, Christ the power of God and*

the wisdom of God. [25] *For the foolishness of God is wiser than men, and the weakness of God is stronger than men.*

[26] *For consider your calling, brothers: not many of you were wise according to worldly standards, not many were powerful, not many were of noble birth.* [27] *But God chose what is foolish in the world to shame the wise; God chose what is weak in the world to shame the strong;* [28] *God chose what is low and despised in the world, even things that are not, to bring to nothing things that are,* [29] *so that no human being might boast in the presence of God.* [30] *And because of him you are in Christ Jesus, who became to us wisdom from God, righteousness and sanctification and redemption,* [31] *so that, as it is written, 'Let the one who boasts, boast in the Lord.'*

1 Corinthians 1

The biggest issue in the church at Corinth was that there was too much Corinth in the Corinthians. That is, the church was corrupted and infected and infused with the worldliness of its surrounding culture.

Too Much Corinth in the Corinthians (1:1–17)

Corinth was a big, successful and strategic city, a port at the centre of some vitally important trade routes, and with multitudes of wealthy and important people passing through all the time. It was a place steeped in power and wealth.

A glitzy, glamorous place of entertainment—including all those types of entertainment one usually finds in port cities. It was a city full of temples and temple prostitution and sexual promiscuity of every conceivable kind, heterosexual and homosexual. It was New York, Amsterdam, London.

It also had something of the Las Vegas or Hollywood about it. A city of bright lights and big dreams and money and celebrity. And the church? Well, the church had all those things too, sadly. Too interested in looking good, in what's impressive, in sex, and in knowledge, and in power.

It was a spiritual church we learn in 1 Corinthians 1 verse 7—not lacking in any spiritual gift. Full of gifted, talented people. But it was also a split church. That's the key thing to notice in the first section of the passage above.

Paul appeals to them to be united, because he's heard that basically they have split into factions. Verse 12 … 'What I mean is that each one of you says, "I follow Paul", or "I follow Apollos", or "I follow Cephas", or "I follow Christ". They were divided and at each other's throats, vying for supremacy.

Now, perhaps we've been used to applying 1 Corinthians to other people, other churches—to Pentecostal churches for example, because they seem to share with the Corinthians an over-emphasis on spiritual gifts and what the scholars call 'over-realized eschatology'—thinking we have more now than we really do. Or to liberal churches, because they seem to share the Corinthian obsession with embracing transgressive sex. Or to divided churches who should all just get along. Or to churches with clever people in them, who are tempted to get puffed up by knowledge as Paul intimates that the Corinthians were.

But we ought to be clear that there is more than enough Corinthian spirit to go around. It has infected those churches that are decidedly non-charismatic, and explicitly non-liberal, just as much as all the others. Perhaps more so, because we've been lulled into thinking this really all applies to someone else.

I used to work in a church in a successful, strategic City. And we considered ourselves blessed in various ways, spiritually. And I'm sure we were—'not lacking in any spiritual gift.'

But I think it's just possible that there was also too much of 'The City' in that City church sometimes. In me too, of course. Too much in the way of worldly thinking that we all pick up, consciously or not, from the place in which we live and work. We breathe in the attitudes and prejudices of our surroundings, the ways of speaking, and ways of acting.

So when we see that the church in Corinth could boast of strong, well-educated, wealthy, successful people and leaders—that it was a strategic and important church … we're not a million miles away from the culture of many evangelical churches today, are we?

We're tempted to think of ourselves in all these ways, aren't we? To overvalue the things that the world on our doorstep values; and to undervalue the things which the world looks down on but which God adores.

Every church has to fight against its surrounding culture of course, but none more so than the church encircled by rampant immorality and greed and glamour and power.

There are even signs in 1 Corinthians that they have started to think of themselves as 'the flagship church', perhaps even 'the best church ever'. They thought they were the 'one true beacon of light' that all in the Christian world should imitate. So several times Paul has to remind them, starting in verse 2 of chapter 1, that there are other true churches elsewhere. He reminds them of this several times throughout the letter. For example, in 1 Corinthians 14:36 he rebukes them for their novel and un-Christian practices, saying, 'was it from you that the word of God came? Or are you the only ones it has reached?'

This is a warning that their deeply eccentric and often ungodly behaviour was at risk of making them into a kind of cult, rather than a recognizable part of the history-spanning, worldwide church of Jesus Christ.

Salvation through weakness (1:18–25)

So this is the context of 1 Corinthians chapter 1. And I've spent a few paragraphs reflecting on that because the context informs what Paul says very directly. So let's look at that in more detail.

The first thing Paul reminds this strong and privileged church is that God's salvation comes through *weakness*. Listen again to verse 18 … 'the word of the cross is folly to those who are perishing, but to us who are being saved it is the power of God.'

There is a big emphasis throughout this section of the letter on power and weakness, wisdom and folly. What he's getting at is that things are not always as they seem. To the world's eyes, and to worldly Christian eyes, the cross is frankly stupid. It's weak and pathetic and a little bit embarrassing. Especially in that culture where crucifixion was something you just didn't talk about, it was so disgusting and barbaric and low.

That's how it looked to the chattering classes of Corinth. But for those with eyes to see, the cross is the power of God to save us. There's the hint that we need the idea of penal substitution to be always at the centre. We need to be *saved* from something, from God's righteous anger against our sin, and the cross is the way in which we're saved from that.

But Paul does not dwell on that thought here. Instead, he deconstructs the world's rejection of the cross. God said 'I will destroy the wisdom of the wise' (verse 19). I will do something that will just not compute with the cleverest human beings. The wise man, the scribe, even in verse 20 the religious expert and theologian. The philosopher and debater—none could have predicted it and none will understand it.

Instead they will, like so many celebrity atheists and atheist buses these days, scoff at the very thought of God and at the weakness of it all. They'll say it's so petty, it's so trivial, it's so local, it's so earth-bound, it's so unworthy.

How can a man dying as a criminal, nailed up on a piece of wood, naked before the crowds, be anything special or anything to me?

I guess the Corinthians were pretty uncomfortable when people said that sort of thing, and mocked their new-found faith. And one reaction we sometimes have is to hide the shame and apparent powerlessness of the cross. We do it, for instance, intellectually. We want to grasp the *logic* of God, to see *behind* what's going on at the cross and consider God's plan just in the abstract or the long term, and not in the blood and the guts and the pain.

But that is to miss something vitally important. Seeing through the cross to what's behind it—focusing just on 'the mechanics of atonement'—*can* be a way of avoiding looking directly at it, in all its weakness, ugliness, powerlessness, and silliness. Sometimes our doctrinal defensiveness can be just another form of *self*-defence—if we can neatly fold the cross into a nice orderly framework of thinking, then it won't hurt us. It won't challenge us. We've got it sussed.

A theologian of the cross has to look at the cross *as it is*, not look behind it. As verse 23 says, the message of Christ crucified is a stumbling block to Jews and folly to Gentiles. But sometimes as Christians, although we know somehow that it's the power of God and the wisdom of God we don't like it, we don't want it to be weak and stupid. Or rather, perhaps, we don't want people to think *we* are weak and stupid.

That's what was going on in Corinth I think. They were far too interested in outward appearance. After all, the word of the cross and the way of the cross were nonsensical in their environment. Can you imagine the PR men in Corinth chatting it over with Jesus? 'Not a good marketing strategy for your product, old boy, dying on a cross. Might work with some weak-minded folks who need a crutch and an inspiring example of suffering. But not here in Corinth. Gotta be more upbeat old chap. Go for the glory rather than the *gory*. That'll work better here.'

Which of course was exactly the strategy the devil had offered Jesus. When he tempted him in the desert he offered Jesus all the glory, all the kingdoms of the world, without a cross, without pain, without suffering. But he chose a different way. He turned down the chance of conventional power and influence when it was offered to him on a plate. And he achieved our salvation and glory for himself, seated on a throne made of wood and nails, and covered in his own blood, sweat, and tears.

But the Corinthian idea of success, and too often the evangelical idea of success is measured in terms of worldly indicators isn't it? Numbers, style, popularity, money, number of franchises opened in the last 10 years. Someone once quipped that 'we count people because people count.' But is that really the reason that we do it?

Hard as it is, 1 Corinthians is telling us here that we're not meant to be successful by worldly standards. We are meant to be faithful by biblical standards, like Jesus. And those two things can be implacably opposed to each other:

success and faithfulness. The way of the cross looks foolish to people who are perishing. But if you want to be saved, this is how.

I've pondered a lot why Paul talks here about the cross and wisdom and strength and success just after introducing the problem of all the divisions in Corinth. Are the two halves of chapter 1 somehow related to each other? What's the connection between the Corinthian divisions and the weakness of the cross?

I think perhaps he's showing them that if they—if we—had a better grip on the foolishness of the cross, *that* would deal with the factionalism, the aggressive sectarian spirit that so often invades the church in places like Corinth.

Now, no doubt there must be divisions, in one way. We'll always have disagreements on things. And they will force us to think the issues through and see who is right. As Paul says later in chapter 11, no doubt there must be factions among us in order that those who are genuine may be recognized (11:19).

But what they were doing in Corinth was just blatant one-upmanship. They were playing ecclesiastical power-politics, using all their worldly skills to make sure their group came out on top.

The Apollos group, the Paul group, the Cephas group, and the group that said it was just following Christ and didn't like all those theological discussions. As one commentator says, they were probably the most sanctimonious, self-righteous, of the lot. Everyone tried to make themselves look good and their opponents look wrong.

But that's not the way to win in *God's* world—a world where salvation is achieved through weakness on a cross. Might does not make right. Indeed, if our knee-jerk reaction to any threat to the power of our group is to puff our chests out and fight—then as Christians we have already lost. Because we haven't understood what the cross is really all about, says Paul. That kind of in-fighting shows how little we've understood the cross.

But I'm afraid we often despise weakness in our church subculture, don't we? Our macho evangelicalism, where doubt and darkness and sorrow are excluded from our horizons because 'we must be strong. We must have a stiff upper lip. We mustn't appear weak, or worse … insignificant.' In our worst moments, we're sorely tempted to talk ourselves up and to talk others down. So we feel we have significance, especially in the eyes of the world, the press, and the Telly.

Salvation for the weak (1:26–31)

And that brings us to the second point here. To those who are worried about being thought insignificant, Paul says salvation is *for* the weak. The word of the cross is a message for those mentioned in verse 26. 'Not many of you were wise according to worldly standards, not many of you were powerful, not many were of noble birth. But God chose what is foolish to shame the wise. God chose what is weak in the world to shame the strong.'

It doesn't say 'not any'. If you're clever or powerful or have blue blood in your veins you can still be saved. I think it was the Countess of Huntingdon in the 18th century who said she was saved by the letter 'm'. It says, 'not many' of you were of noble birth—rather than, 'not any'. So being a mover and a shaker, or having a PhD is not *necessarily* a bad thing—but being well-bred or well-qualified doesn't make someone more spiritual. Why do we instinctively assume it does, when we meet people in the Christian world like that?

The point is clear, isn't it? *How* does God save?—through weakness, through the cross. *Who* does he save?—weak and insignificant people. God doesn't choose people for their worldly qualifications. *His* interest in us doesn't depend on how *others* rate us, how many Facebook friends or followers we have on Twitter. Salvation is for the weak and the despised.

And that drives successful people crazy, doesn't it? Middle-class, social climbing, ambitious people do not like to be told that to be saved they must lower themselves, and join a bunch of people—the church—who, let's be frank, are really nothing special. And in fact are looked down up on.

Unless of course it's an opportunity for them to shine and come out on top. That's a different matter. 'Cream always rises to the top' after all, so perhaps joining this Christian bunch is a way for me to climb up further and enhance my reputation. If I can excel and get ahead in the church and be a leader, then that's OK. As long as I don't have to be *too* keen on it all.' Is that just an Anglican disease?

I think this attitude was probably behind some of the factionalism and divisions in Corinth. We know from chapter 11 that when they got together in church the strong despised the weak and took advantage of them for their own gratification.

But Paul is saying right at the start that this has to be wrong, because the weak cross saves weak people, who don't need to prove they are strong and together to be accepted and loved by God.

I know that in many churches there are lots of very competent people—Christians who make lesser mortals feel that we're never quite good enough, and that we're minnows in the fishpond as Christians compared to their shining example. Super-Christians whose capacity for service of God seems to be on another level from ours.

That could be very intimidating! We should thank God for his gift of grace to such people, to empower them for such efforts. But we don't *all* have to be like that. We are not all programmed to excel and to lead. In the church of Jesus Christ, the despised and rejected one, everyone is welcome no matter how strong or educated or successful you are. There is level ground at the foot of the cross. No pedestals. And no ladders to climb.

So I want to say to Christians who are weak and struggling and intimidated and feel insignificant—church is for you. What Jesus did on the cross was for you. Not just for the happy, strong, beautiful, self-sufficient people. But for all who are burdened and struggling—and quiet, and eccentric, and odd.

And let's face it, actually lots of us who on the surface appear self-sufficient and strong and 'normal' are aching underneath with a whole host of anxieties and insecurities and weaknesses. That should be obvious, every time a rich, famous celebrity commits suicide or ends up in rehab.

We need to be honest with ourselves, with God, and with others, rather than projecting an image of ourselves as Christians which does no honour to the crucified one who knows what it is to cry and say, 'My God, my God, why have you forsaken me?'

Jesus knows how that feels. He knows our weakness. So we don't have to collapse under the strain of having to appear together, or having to compete in the game of who's the best and keenest Christian. Our saviour was crucified, crushed to death by the weight of our sin and God's wrath against it, so that we can be free of that pressure to perform.

Let him who boasts, boast in the Lord and what he did for worms like us on that cross. And leave in the past the human boasting and measuring of ourselves against others.

So, 1 Corinthians 1 shows us that the cross not only saves us. It also powerfully demolishes and deconstructs all our views of what success and failure look like. God's power is made perfect in weakness.

2

Mark 10:32–45

The Cross and Service

A nd they were on the road, going up to Jerusalem, and Jesus was walking ahead of them. And they were amazed, and those who followed were afraid. And taking the twelve again, he began to tell them what was to happen to him, [33] saying, 'See, we are going up to Jerusalem, and the Son of Man will be delivered over to the chief priests and the scribes, and they will condemn him to death and deliver him over to the Gentiles. [34] And they will mock him and spit on him, and flog him and kill him. And after three days he will rise.'

[35] And James and John, the sons of Zebedee, came up to him and said to him, 'Teacher, we want you to do for us whatever we ask of you.' [36] And he said to them, 'What do you want me to do for you?' [37] And they said to him, 'Grant us to sit, one at your right hand and one at your left, in your glory.' [38] Jesus said to them, 'You do not know what you are asking. Are you able to drink the cup that I drink, or to be baptized with the baptism with which I am baptized?' [39] And they said to him, 'We are able.' And

Jesus said to them, 'The cup that I drink you will drink, and with the baptism with which I am baptized, you will be baptized, ⁴⁰ but to sit at my right hand or at my left is not mine to grant, but it is for those for whom it has been prepared.' ⁴¹ And when the ten heard it, they began to be indignant at James and John. ⁴² And Jesus called them to him and said to them, 'You know that those who are considered rulers of the Gentiles lord it over them, and their great ones exercise authority over them. ⁴³ But it shall not be so among you. But whoever would be great among you must be your servant,⁴⁴ and whoever would be first among you must be slave of all. ⁴⁵ For even the Son of Man came not to be served but to serve, and to give his life as a ransom for many.'

Mark 10:32–45

In this chapter, we're going to look at the cross and service. This story in Mark's Gospel may well sound familiar. We may know that lovely verse 45, 'even the Son of Man came not to be served but to serve and give his life as a ransom for many.'

And of course there it is, the idea that Jesus died in our place, as the ransom price to save us from sin and death. But much as we could dwell on that glorious thought, there's something else for us here as well, which we must not overlook. All this talk of Jesus dying and serving was a bit of a shock to his first disciples. We could easily miss the outrage because we're so used to the idea that Jesus was crucified. But to them, this came as something of a surprise.

Longing for Glory

Why was the cross such a surprise? Jesus' disciples were longing for glory. That's what they thought would happen when the Messiah came—they were longing for glory.

To give us a bit of context, Mark's Gospel begins by establishing who Jesus is. So in the first 8 chapters we hear about his miracles and his teaching, and everyone's amazed. Then in chapter 8 Jesus asks his disciples in verse 27, 'Who do people say that I am?' They check with the focus groups. But then he turns the question round and asks them directly—'Who do *you* say that I am?'

Peter speaks up and says 'You're the Christ'. That is, you're the Messiah, the saviour promised to us by God for centuries. Our king. The special one sent from God.

And that's the turning point. Because now they've got that, Jesus goes on to teach them what being the Messiah really means. So as soon as they know who he is, he tells them what he's come to do. 'And he began to teach them that the Son of Man [that's his name for himself] must suffer many things and be rejected by the elders and the chief priests and the scribes [the religious establishment] and be killed, and after three days rise again.'

For Peter, this just does not compute. Rejection and death were not on his schedule. So Peter thinks he'd better have a word with Jesus and set him straight about what being the Christ means.

Get the irony of it—a feeble human being telling his creator off for getting something wrong! And for misunderstanding the Bible no less—'Haven't you read that when the Messiah comes he's going to rule the world in power and glory, Jesus? Being rejected by the establishment ... well, maybe. But then showing them what's what and getting your own back of course. Not being rejected and then *killed*! That's failure. That's weakness. That's ... pointless.'

Peter has his eyes so firmly fixed on the glory that he's forgotten the cross. God's way of doing things is completely different to what we might expect. So Jesus accuses Peter of speaking for the opposition: 'Get behind me, Satan! You're not setting your mind on the things of God, but on the things of man.' Going for glory is the devil's department.

Jesus tells Peter that if he wants to save his life and gain the world (which he clearly does!), he has to give it all up and follow Jesus to the cross. Which is not quite what Peter had planned.

His idea was to give up his little fishing boat and swap it for a chauffeur-driven chariot. But now Jesus is talking about rejection and death *first*, before he comes 'in the glory of his Father with the holy angels' (verse 38). 'Why can't we just have the glory now?' he no doubt wondered, as many of us do.

This happens three times in Mark chapters 8–10. Jesus tells them straight—they're going to kill me. And three times his disciples just don't seem to get it. How could something so bad happen to a man who can walk on water, heal the sick with a word, and give orders to the wind and waves? He's untouchable, surely?

But they do get the 'coming in glory with the holy angels' stuff. Now *that* they can understand. So in chapter 9 verse 34, they argue with each other about which of them is the greatest. Vying for position in the king's inner circle, because they sense that Jesus is on the way up and he'll be taking them all with him into his council and cabinet to rule the world.

Then, for the third time, Jesus tells them in Mark chapter 10, 'We're going to Jerusalem and I'm going to be condemned, mocked, spat on, flogged, and killed. Oh yes, and after that I'll rise again.' Again, all pretty clear and gruesome and unpleasant. But what is it the disciples hear?

James and John, the sons of Zebedee, said to him, 'Grant us to sit, one at your right hand and one at your left *in your glory.*' (Mark 10:37). Typical isn't it? They only see the glory! They've *forgotten the cross.*

They want to be the left hand man and the right hand man of the top man. And they're not ashamed to push themselves forward.

Now, I want the glory too. Don't you? This world *can* be good, but it can also be disappointing, and shabby, and messy. Our lives seem to have so much potential, but things are also strangely 'out of focus' and not quite right. Even our best moments are often tainted with some sadness or grief or fear. Every silver lining has a cloud.

There are signs that we were made for something better than this, that this is not the way the world is meant to be. We long for something better—we hope that it's just around the corner with a new job maybe or a new relationship, or a new gadget, or a new house, or a new Government perhaps.

But it's not. We long for glory and perfection and a new order—but only when Jesus comes back in power and glory with his holy angels will we actually one day get that. Yet still we often persist in trying to get ahead, so we can get the glory now.

It would be good if this was just an attitude that Jesus' followers fell into in the early days, *before* the cross happened and put them all straight. But it's not, is it? There's a guy mentioned in one of the disciple John's letters, later on in the Bible. He was an early Christian leader called Diotrephes. John, who obviously knew a thing or two about ambition himself in his youth, writes this:

'I have written something to the church, but Diotrephes, *who likes to put himself first*, does not acknowledge our authority.' (3 John 9).

Diotrephes loved to be first. He liked the limelight. And the power and the glory. He wouldn't allow any rivals to get in his way or share the leadership—even the apostle John, the specially commissioned ambassador of the Lord Jesus Christ.

So he kept John out of the church, and slandered his friends. Why? Because they challenged his powerbase. He did so love to be first, and to throw his weight around.

You won't have to scrabble around for long to think of examples of the same thing today. But if you draw a blank, just go online. There are plenty of Diotrephes lookalikes in ministry today, calling themselves 'leaders.'

And that's the same evil impulse that led James and John and Peter to rebuke Jesus for talking about the cross.

He Lowered Himself

In contrast to that, Jesus patiently taught his disciples that there is a better way. Focusing on the glory they forgot the cross. But Jesus, for the joy that was set before him, lowered himself and died.

Jesus was very different to Diotrephes, wasn't he? And to James and John. He was in very nature God, and yet he didn't consider his divine status something to be held onto jealously for his own profit and benefit. Instead, he made himself nothing. He became a servant, he humbled himself, and was obedient all the way to death.

That's not what we expect from great men, is it? I know there are stories of kings and millionaires who go out among 'the common people' to get their hands dirty for a bit. But those are just fairy stories aren't they? Real people with real power and wealth don't do that sort of thing for very long. They don't lower themselves—unless they have to, unless it's for a photo opportunity or a TV reality show.

Except Jesus. He said to his disciples in Mark 10:42, 'You know that those who are considered rulers of the Gentiles lord it over them, and their great ones exercise authority over them. But it shall not be so among you. But whoever would be great among you must be your servant, and whoever would be first among you must be slave of all. For even the Son of Man came not to be served but to serve, and to give his life as a ransom for many.'

Even the Son of Man. That name, Son of Man, was given to someone in a vision in the Old Testament book of Daniel. And it says there that to this Son of Man will be 'given dominion and glory and a kingdom, that all peoples, nations, and languages should serve him; his dominion is an everlasting dominion, which shall not pass away, and his kingdom one that shall not be destroyed' (Daniel 7:13–14). *There's* the Son of Man, the Son of God, being given what he deserves.

But before he gets that, we have here the one who created and upholds the universe with his powerful word, spending quality time with a bunch of Galilean peasants. The one who designed the Orion nebula and the Grand Canyon and Niagara Falls, sawing a bit of wood to make a table in his carpenter's shop for some old lady in Nazareth. The hands which cast stars into space, surrendering to the cruel iron nails that pierced his hands and feet, for us.

Have you got the shock yet? While everybody else with even a sniff at greatness and glory puffs their chest out and pushes their way through, Jesus laid aside his crown, washed his disciples' smelly feet, and then let the worst kind of religious hypocrites, snobs, and elitist bully-boys make him into a scapegoat.

Jesus was very clear about the cross he had to bear. A real cross, with real nails, and real blood, and real suffocating death. He did it to bear the punishment for our sins, and also to show the world the way to true greatness.

Are you being served?

So how are we to apply this to ourselves? It would be easy to start by saying 'Jesus says we must serve each other'. Love one another, be nice to one another. But I think that misses the most important point.

Yes, he left us an example, and we'll look at that in a moment. But he also came to serve us. To wash our feet, to be the atoning sacrifice for the sins of the world. So the first question we have to ask ourselves is not 'are we serving each other?' But rather, if you'll forgive me, the question is 'Are you being served?'

Have we let Jesus serve us, or are we stubborn and proud like Peter, not wanting to accept that we need to wash our feet (so to speak), or that *Jesus* has to do it? That we stink as far as God is concerned, and only *he* can wash us clean?

Our biggest need according to the Bible is that we need to *be* served, by Jesus. And that's not an easy thing for us to accept. Our culture tells us that we need to be strong independent people who can stand on their own two feet. But Jesus says, we can't. We need him.

For a start we need to be ransomed, he says. 'Even the Son of Man came not be served but to serve and give his life as a ransom for many.'

What were we ransomed from? Peter himself writes it in one of his letters—'you were ransomed from the futile ways inherited from your forefathers, not with perishable things such as silver or gold, but with the precious blood of Christ' (1 Peter 1:18–19).

Without Jesus, we're stuck just going round and round in the cycle of futility, always ending up making the same mistakes as previous generations, falling into the same old mess. Jesus can rescue us from that spiral. And from the eternal consequences of our God-rejecting hearts, from which all that vanity ultimately springs.

Some people do recognize this. They're here in Mark's record. He's placed them deliberately in the middle of Jesus' teaching about the cross.

So we see the *desperate father* in Mark chapter 9 verse 24. He brought his sick child to Jesus, at his wits end. Something was causing his son immense pain and suffering, and nothing had worked. He knew he needed Jesus, to restore his son to him. But he was sceptical, and couldn't quite believe it would work. He begged Jesus to help. Jesus said 'all things are possible for the one who believes.' So he answered in revealing panic, 'I do believe—help my unbelief!'

That's the cry of a heart that knows it needs to be served by Jesus. I do believe. I want to believe. Help me to believe. He knows he can't even control his own heart, that he needs help at the deepest level of his being, to enable him to trust in Christ, and see his boy made well again.

A desperate father finds hope. And children too can find blessing. In chapter 10 verse 14 we hear that 'to such belongs the kingdom of God.' The kingdom of God is populated by children, who never made it into adulthood. And also by those who know they need to come the same trusting, childlike way. The kingdom of God belongs to those who come to be served by Jesus, humbly, without deceit, without a front or an agenda. Just come to Jesus without the mask you wear for other people, and you'll be blessed.

And then further on, there's the blind beggar in Mark 10 verse 46. He calls out again and again, 'Jesus, have mercy on me! Jesus, give me my sight!' He knows he needs to be served. He's trapped in a darkened world and needs help to get around.

For him the world is a frightening place, and a pitiless confusion. Passers-by told him to shut up and stop bothering Jesus. But he kept on asking and didn't give up, even if it meant being socially unacceptable.

These three incidents are put here in Mark's account to show us what it looks like to be served by Jesus. We need his help to give us faith. We need his help to heal us. We need his blessing. We need his mercy. We need our sight back, so we can see him as he truly is: the Son of Man who came not to be served—as he deserved—but to serve.

Drinking the Poisoned Chalice?

But finally, we ought to look at what all this teaches us about serving one another as Jesus served us. Jesus asked James and John whether they could drink the cup he was about to drink—a reference to his impending death. Or be baptized with his baptism—another reference to his death.

To drink the cup he drinks, of course, means we have to take up the fatal cross like he did, and follow him in the way of service and sacrifice for others.

Yet that's such a counter-intuitive thing to do—it goes against all our instincts to drink poison even if someone tells us it will be alright in the end. And in the same way it's against our instincts to give up our rights and what we think we deserve, in order to serve others and put ourselves out for them.

It says in Matthew's Gospel that James and John weren't the first ones to approach Jesus and ask to be at his side in glory. Their mother, Mrs Zebedee, approached Jesus first and asked if he'd do something for her boys.

As an ambitious mother, she wanted for them what most mothers want for their kids—leadership, glory, good things. It's what our schools promise to produce, and what we secretly or openly long for—fame, celebrity, power, privilege. Or other things that we never had but hope we can help them achieve.

But Jesus says none of that really matters. So here's something to chat about if you have children: how does Jesus' agenda for costly service of others affect what we as Christians want for our kids? Are our ambitions for them like those of Mrs Zebedee, or like those of Jesus?

Secondly, all this has something to say to those who would be leaders themselves. What does drinking the poisoned chalice, the cup of service that Jesus offers us, look like for potential leaders in the church? I think Derek Tidball says it brilliantly, when he writes in one of his commentaries:

The danger of much of today's Christianity, with its concentration on major gatherings and celebrity speakers, is that it sets wrong aspirations before emerging Christian leaders. Some see the glamour and glitz and want to have a prominent place in the celebration event or on the big platform before they are ready. They do not see, and they fail to grasp, the significance of serving God faithfully in the unremarkable, small, and routine work that characterises most service for God.[1]

I fear he's right. We need to say to ourselves, 'Don't look for power and prestige. Because even the Son of Man came not to be served but to serve, and to give his life for others.' Ministry is not about you being fulfilled. It's about being useful to the master, ready for any good work he might set you.

We need to go do something which nobody else can be bothered to do, some kind of unremarkable or routine service for God which nobody sees, and which we'll never make into a sermon illustration. The more we do those small things with contentment and joy, the more qualified we'll be for any other kind of ministry.

We definitely shouldn't long for a position in a famous, flagship church. My wife told me that another minister's wife once said at a conference that her greatest aspiration was for her husband to be in charge of a big, thriving, famous church. We were actually working in such a place at the time (though I had not applied for the job or ever expected to be there!). But that open confession of naked ambition was a shock.

Such places are full of sinners who need serving too, of course. And full of great opportunities for service. But serving in a place like that is not only an opportunity to learn. It's a huge temptation to yearn, to long for the wrong things, to dream about ourselves, and to be led astray by the subtle enticements and allurements of reputation and worldly pride. It's noble to want to make the biggest impact we can for the gospel. But it's probably better for most of us, especially for the health of our souls, if that's in a place that nobody's ever heard of.

It is harder to resist that sinful craving for glory, or even to see it as wrong, if one is surrounded by the kind of culture in which people like Mrs Zebedee and Peter and Diotrephes seem to be so prominent. We need to be careful that we don't adopt the attitude, all too common in those who see ministry as a 'profession', that says 'I'm happy to be a slave, as long as I can be an important one.'

The question we're left with here is very simple: would you give up everything *you* have, and everything you'd *like* to have, to follow Jesus to the cross?

It may not be glamorous. But in the end, even for Jesus, it's the only way to true and lasting glory.

1 Peter 2:12–25

The Cross and Suffering

*B*eloved, I urge you as sojourners and exiles to abstain from the passions of the flesh, which wage war against your soul. ¹² Keep your conduct among the Gentiles honourable, so that when they speak against you as evildoers, they may see your good deeds and glorify God on the day of visitation.

¹³ Be subject for the Lord's sake to every human institution, whether it be to the emperoras supreme, ¹⁴ or to governors as sent by him to punish those who do evil and to praise those who do good. ¹⁵ For this is the will of God, that by doing good you should put to silence the ignorance of foolish people. ¹⁶ Live as people who are free, not using your freedom as a cover-up for evil, but living as servants of God. ¹⁷ Honour everyone. Love the brotherhood. Fear God. Honour the emperor.

¹⁸ Servants, be subject to your masters with all respect, not only to the good and gentle but also to the unjust. ¹⁹ For this is a gracious thing, when, mindful of God, one endures sorrows

while suffering unjustly. [20] *For what credit is it if, when you sin and are beaten for it, you endure? But if when you do good and suffer for it you endure, this is a gracious thing in the sight of God.* [21] *For to this you have been called, because Christ also suffered for you, leaving you an example, so that you might follow in his steps.* [22] *He committed no sin, neither was deceit found in his mouth.* [23] *When he was reviled, he did not revile in return; when he suffered, he did not threaten, but continued entrusting himself to him who judges justly.* [24] *He himself bore our sins in his body on the tree, that we might die to sin and live to righteousness. By his wounds you have been healed.* [25] *For you were straying like sheep, but have now returned to the Shepherd and Overseer of your souls.*

1 Peter 2:11–25

Because the doctrine of Jesus taking the punishment I deserve on the cross has been under attack in recent years, many writers and scholars have focused on it. It may even have become something of a shibboleth in some circles, that needs to be mentioned as often as possible just to prove one's soundness. This can be deeply unhelpful, not least because it can lead to a loss of perspective, and a wider biblical amnesia.

We rightly want to focus on the central core message of the cross, but in doing so we sometimes forget other things that are going on there. I'm not saying that we don't know about these other aspects and applications of the cross. At least, in this chapter we're not looking at something that we've forgotten intellectually. But, rather, we need to look again at something we may easily neglect *practically*.

At the same time as being our penal substitute, Jesus left us an example to follow. His death wasn't simply an illustration of unjust suffering and how to endure it. It was more than that, because we needed more than that. An inspiring role model cannot rescue me from death or from God's judgment. But because it truly and objectively saves me, Jesus' death can also be a pattern for us to follow.

We know in our heads that being a Christian is not about being comfortable in this life, or respected by the world. Yet somehow it is still possible for us to aim for that and long for that, and to miss what the cross tells us about life before heaven, which is sometimes ugly and difficult.

Once again we're thinking here about imitating the Lord Jesus. In the last chapter, Jesus taught us through Mark's Gospel that the way to glory is through being served by Christ and serving others. But in this chapter we need to confront what the Bible says about the cross and suffering.

That makes Peter's first letter to the embattled Christians of ancient Turkey the ideal place for us to be. The context of this letter is one of suffering and persecution. The Christians Peter is writing to are facing the ignorance of foolish people.

The ignorance of foolish people

That's the arresting way that Peter puts it in chapter 2 verse 15, when he tells them 'that by doing good you should put to silence *the ignorance of foolish people.*'

What form was this foolish persecution taking? We can tell quite a lot from the letter. So in verse 12 Peter implies that those who are not Christians are 'speaking against' the believers. We can guess from the way he applies the example of Christ later on in verse 23 that they faced what's called there 'reviling'—that is, insults, verbal abuse, scorn, ridicule, contempt. And there's more of that in chapter 4 too.

People are saying mean and nasty things about Christians. And they are to answer such accusations and slander only by doing good in return.

But they're not just facing harsh words. They're also facing sticks and stones. There's mention in verse 20 of *beatings*. The people addressed here, particularly the Christian slaves, face literal physical discomfort because of their faith in Jesus Christ.

Recently my wife and I watched the film *Twelve Years A Slave*, about a freeman from New York City in 1841 being kidnapped and enslaved in the antebellum Deep South. It was harrowing. The sheer evil of it all was infuriating, and it was meant to be. But I was affected particularly by the ugliness of the beatings which those slaves were forced to endure, and the monstrous injustice of it. That's something of the flavour of the situation these slaves that Peter is addressing in his letter may have faced too. It wasn't pretty or easy. We should not gloss it over or make light of it.

Persecution is ignorant and foolish. It's treating God's own children as if they were the scum of the earth. I don't know what would happen if someone tried to assault or abuse say Prince Charles or Prince Andrew. But there'd be trouble wouldn't there? You can't treat Her Majesty the Queen's children with disrespect and expect to get away with it.

You would only think about doing something like that if you were *ignorant* of who they are, and *foolish* enough not to notice the bodyguards or the prison sentence that awaits you. You'd have to be foolish and ignorant to attack the Queen's heirs.

And in the same way, Peter says when people attack Christians for following Jesus, they really can't be in full possession of their sanity. They must be ignorant and foolish to even try such a thing against those whom Peter calls God's own possession. Attacking people for believing in Jesus is madness—it's reality-denying blindness and stupidity of the very first order.

If you tried to physically or verbally abuse a member of the royal family, I guess a ton of secret service people are going to be on top of you within a few seconds, and the whole weight of the legal system will be pressed into action against you. So what's God going to do about it when *his* children suffer slander or physical 'sorrow' at the hands of foolish and ignorant people?

That's a puzzling question. Because the answer in our immediate experience appears to be … nothing.

No angelic bodyguards flew down from heaven to defend murdered missionaries sent to far off lands with the gospel of peace in days gone by. No thunderbolts were hurled at the extremists who enslaved and murdered and chased away the Christians from central Iraq in summer 2014. No flashes of lightning answer the unjust remarks of those who insult us or wrong us.

So it looks as if God isn't doing anything to help us. And that's a major problem for many people. If God is good and all-powerful, then why doesn't he stop such things? Why not stop ALL injustice and evil at a stroke, so that ignorant and foolish people are put to shame and all wrongs are righted immediately?

There is no easy answer to that. But it can look very much as if God has abandoned us, forsaken us, and left us as Christians to our own devices to suffer the slings and arrows of outrageous fortune and a sea of troubles and insults. Should we take up arms against them? Should we retaliate in kind?

Temptations in the face of suffering

In this period of apparent divine silence, when we face the ignorance of fools, we are confronted with some very big temptations. When faced with slander or sorrow our first temptation is to resist the suffering.

By that I mean we try to stop it, get around it, or evade it. But as with paying tax, avoidance is sort of OK (putting money into a tax-free savings scheme for example)—but evasion is definitely not.

To *evade* persecution means not taking the hit that actually we need to take. So if someone laughs at you for believing in life after death you can evade that sideswipe by saying you *don't* believe in that. If they call you names for being a Bible-basher then you can resist them by denying that you go to that evangelical church or that you listen to their sermons on your iPod. We resist the suffering and aim for comfort and respect from our peers instead.

It's a great temptation to evade persecution that way. Though it's much more honourable to *avoid* persecution, by taking ourselves out of the situation. So leave that place of work where the atmosphere is poisoned against Christianity. Resign from the job where the office joke is you and your faith. Run away from the men with the guns, rather than denying your faith in the hope of saving your life.

Not that resigning and moving away from a hostile work environment was much of an option for the people Peter is writing to. Because from verse 18 onwards he's addressing Christian slaves. Slavery in the ancient world wasn't exactly like the slavery we probably first think of, the enslavement of African men and women in 18th and 19th century Europe and America.

It wasn't restricted to one race enslaving another, for a start, and seems to have been less based on class and education. So a first-century slave *could* be in hard physical manual work, but they could equally well be doctors, engineers, lawyers, accountants, teachers, and secretaries. Like many of us, in good middle-class professions.

But slaves were still stuck with their owners. No chance of handing in their resignation and signing on at the local job centre. And it seems that the slaves Peter was writing to here were not in the enviable situation of some slaves elsewhere—there is nothing here addressed specifically to Christian masters as there is in other letters (e.g. Ephesians, Philemon), so perhaps there weren't any. These Christian slaves had unbelieving masters, or masters who worshipped different gods and goddesses.

The middle section of 1 Peter is all about relating to that non-Christian world which can oppose, hinder, question, or tempt us. Perhaps particularly in work situations then, these slaves would face a second temptation. When faced with ignorant and foolish masters, they would be tempted to rebel, and run away. But Peter tells them in verse 18 to be subject to their masters, to submit to them. Just as Christian citizens and freemen were to submit to the human authorities placed over them in the form of magistrates and emperors. Even if they were not good or kind.

But they'd also be tempted to rebel against God. Peter tells his readers in verse 11 to abstain from the passions of the flesh which wage war against their souls. To fight against sin in their hearts and lives. That's what Christian discipleship is all about.

But if you just stop doing that, rebel against God and submit to the opposition, life becomes a lot easier it seems. We no longer have the internal battles and conflicted emotions that are part and parcel of daily spiritual warfare. Instead of trying by the power of God's Spirit to live godly lives which please and glorify him, we can 'relax and be ourselves'—which invariably means relaxing our moral standards and becoming less than what God intended us to be in Christ.

Many Christians find that verbal abuse can be a very effective tactic for the devil to use in this regard. Because it makes us feel victimised—'but I'm in the right! How dare they say or do that against me because of what I believe, how can they be so horrible!' And pretty soon we're sinfully angry, and painfully self-obsessed, and walking right into Satan's delicious little trap.

He provokes us through other people's mocking, to see what is really in us. And let's be honest, often we end up rebelling against God when that happens, because at heart we don't like being different or standing out from the crowd. The only thing we want to repress is the nagging voice of conscience.

And so our eyes are refocused. We redeploy our mental and spiritual energies. I stop looking at God, and in a situation of suffering I start looking at my persecutor, my enemy … and at myself. I seethe inside about the injustice, and stroke my wounded pride.

I concentrate on all *their* faults and foolishness, and soothe the pain by rehearsing in the shower all the conversations I'm going to have with those people who've wronged me. 'I'll say this, and this, and this. And that will shut them up …'

Effortlessly we slide into thinking about retaliation. Revenge. When we face insults, especially if we're good with words or have a colourful vocabulary, it's very tempting to strike back isn't it? Educated people can be very good at the withering put down and the contemptuous reply, which makes us feel good. But it's not the way that Jesus responded.

So faced with injustice and persecution of various kinds, our temptation is to resist, rebel, refocus, and retaliate. How does Peter pastor the people he's writing to, as these thoughts swirl round their heads? Knowing what temptations they felt when faced with foolish and ignorant opposition, Peter sets before these Christians the example of Christ on the cross.

Look to the suffering Christ

Peter says in verse 20 that they are to keep doing good even if they suffer for it. For 'to this you have been called, because Christ also suffered for you, leaving you an example, so that you might follow in his steps.'

The word he uses there for 'example' is a word also used in the school classroom. It's like a stencil to help children to write, or a join-the-dots alphabet which children go over in pencil to learn how to write their letters. Christ left us the sketch, the outline, the template, for life as a Christian in a hostile environment. And in case we've forgotten, the stencil is cross-shaped.

So let's look at the dots, to see what Peter tells us about Christ's example of suffering on the cross. And then we'll go over it in pen for ourselves and see how we're meant to write our lives in imitation of Jesus.

Jesus suffered *sinlessly*. That's the first thing Peter tells us. Verse 22 says, 'He committed no sin and no deceit was found in his mouth.' It's a direct quote from Isaiah chapter 53 in the Old Testament, a prophecy about the death of the Messiah which Peter alludes to several times in these few verses.

When he was arrested on trumped-up charges, the Lord Jesus did not complain or resist. He didn't strike back. No sinful thoughts ran around in his head, no sinful words or deeds.

You may remember that in the Old Testament Temple, you were only allowed to offer a spotless, perfect animal as a sacrifice to God. Well, here he is—the one who fulfils all the prophecies and patterns of the Old Testament. And he truly was a lamb without blemish, the spotless sacrifice without a sin to his name. So he could take our sins, and die from the weight on his shoulders, while he offers us his whole and perfect obedience, to wrap around ourselves in return.

As an example of his sinless suffering, we observe here his *silence*. So Peter says 'when he was reviled (insulted) he did not revile in return. When he suffered, he did not threaten.'

I would have, wouldn't you? If I were God incarnate, the maker of heaven and earth in a human body being assaulted by these puny little creatures, the second they tried to bang the nails into my left hand I'd have raised my right hand and squeezed the living daylights out of them, turned them back into dust, or thrown them into the air like Gandalf does in *Lord of the Rings*.

Not so with Jesus. The one who taught us to turn the other cheek, lets them hammer in the nails: first the left hand, then the right hand, then the feet, and lift him up. Without even bleating.

I might have whispered to the soldier, 'Just you wait 'till I come back from the dead.' But Jesus prayed 'Father forgive them, for they know not what they do.'

He suffered sinlessly, and silently. But also *safely*. That's the force of the end of verse 23 I think. 'He continued entrusting himself to him who judges justly.' He knew what was happening wasn't right. How could it be right to crucify the Lord of Glory, God the Son?

And he knew what God the Father had promised on the other side of death. The Scriptures are clear that he would see the light of life and be satisfied, and would sit at God's right hand. So he trusted in that promise, and endured the pain for now, confident that when it was all over, everything would change.

I think I probably would have caved in if I were being crucified. I'd have promised the soldiers anything if they'd just let me go. I'd have promised the leaders I'd disappear, or join forces with them, if only they'd smile on me and vote to keep me in this world. But Jesus looked up to his Father and yearned for no other smile but his.

That's what kept him going. He didn't care what the world thought of him. Whatever black clouds faced him here he longed only for the sunshine of God's face. He looked to the future when God will judge the living and the dead, and right all wrongs. And he knew that whatever happened now, he would be safe then, because of God's promise.

I noticed that in *Twelve Years a Slave*, a repeated refrain that there would one day be a day of reckoning, a day when scores are settled, a day when people have to answer for their sins, a time when wrongs will be made right. It is a constant theme which propels the film forward, not just to the final rescue of the main character, nor even to the abolition of slavery in the Civil War which followed soon after. But a day when those who evade justice in this life will be finally brought to book (unlike the kidnappers and enslavers from the film's true story, who never were). On that day, those who suffer unjustly will be free.

What that film could only hint at, Jesus knew as a solid reality. He entrusted himself to the one who judges justly, his heavenly Father, while his enemies did their worst.

He suffered sinlessly, silently, and safely. And he did it *for our sins*. That aspect is clearly here. 'By his wounds we are healed,' says Peter, healed from our backsliding and straying from God. 'He bore our sins in his body on the tree', and in another echo of Isaiah 53, 'each of us had turned to our own way, but the Lord has laid on *Jesus* the iniquity of us all.'

We need that. Because an example alone doesn't save us. It may be inspiring but it gives me no power to reform myself. And it doesn't deal with my biggest problem—which is that God is angry with my sin and must, as the moral judge of the universe, punish me for it. And yet,'Christ suffered once for sins, the righteous for the unrighteous, that he might bring us to God' (1 Peter 3:18).

So although my temptation in the midst of any suffering I face is to resist and rebel and retaliate, Christ suffered sinlessly, he suffered silently, and he suffered safely, for my sins.

So the final point has to be this: follow the shepherd.

Follow the shepherd

Over the years I've learned that a great leader doesn't ask someone else to do something that he wouldn't be prepared to do himself. It's leadership lesson number one, I think. And Jesus is a great leader. He's done it all, even unto death.

Now he asks us, as our shepherd and overseer (our pastor and bishop you could translate it), to also endure suffering—sinlessly, silently, and safely.

When it gets tough, when we feel like we're facing impossible choices between godliness and getting ahead, we can't say, 'But Lord, you've no idea what it's like.' Oh, he has. He knows. And he kept his priorities straight, and he kept doing good.

So we must follow *sinlessly*—*he* died that *we* might die to sin and live for righteousness says chapter 2 verse 24. He shows us how to wage war against the passions of our flesh, which drag us in every direction but back to the cross.

We follow *silently*. We endure the sorrows and suffering and slander whether it's justified by our actions (as it sometimes is because we're not perfect), or whether it's completely unjustified and unfair. That's what he did. So 'consider him who endured from sinners such hostility against himself, so that you will not grow weary or fainthearted' (Hebrews 12:3).

Consider him. Follow him. Because you know that's the safest way to go. We must as 1 Peter 2 verse 19 says, be mindful of God. We must entrust *everything* to him who judges justly. Not only ourselves, but also those who oppose us. We must entrust them to God too, and the judgment we think they deserve. We don't have to take matters into our own hands. We can trust the Father to see to it, fairly and without partiality.

Peter tells us that there will be 'a day of visitation.' A day of reckoning. The Lord is coming to judge the world. And on that day, Jesus said, everyone will have to account for every last word they've spoken. Including everyone who's ever said a hurtful, offensive, or sneering word against those whom God has loved. From 'Loser!' to 'Jesus freak!' to 'Don't be so repressed!' to 'Kill her.'

Whatever has been done in secret, Jesus said, will come out. And there is no partiality with God. People who can get away with injustice here because of their power, influence, connections, or status will not be able to do so before God. In heaven every playing field is a level playing field.

So we can leave the seething resentment, and forget the shower-time rehearsals and replays of competitive conversations. Leave it all to God. He will have the last word, even if you weren't able to, and you never see justice done in this life.

If we suffer unjustly, mindful of God and this promise, verses 19 and 20 tell us 'this is a gracious thing in his sight.' That's an unusual way to say it, but what he's getting at is that there will be a reward, a grace, a gift at the end. Chapter 1 of Peter's letter tells us that we have a living hope, an inheritance and a salvation ready to be revealed. If only we continue in the way.

As I close, do you remember the story of Hansel and Gretel? Two young children are taken out into the forest one day and then abandoned by their father, who can't afford to look after them anymore.

But they discover that this is going to happen just before they leave home, so they pick up lots of white pebbles. And as their father leads them into the darkest parts of the forest they drop the pebbles every so often, to mark their way back home.

Well, I've missed out the wicked stepmother, the botched attempt to use breadcrumbs instead of pebbles, and the evil witch with the gingerbread house, but we can save that for another time. What I'm getting at is that we may feel sometimes like Hansel and Gretel. We may feel we have been abandoned by our Father, forgotten. Left alone to face a merciless and dangerous and unjust world, to fend for ourselves, to suffer, and to die.

But our Father in heaven is not like the father in Hansel and Gretel. For some reason we do find ourselves, for a little while, suffering and straining—far away from home, as aliens and strangers in a world which doesn't have our best interests at heart.

We may never understand his reasons for bringing us to this place. But before he brought us here, the Father sent his Son out first, to suffer and to die in this vale of tears.

And as he goes to the cross, Jesus leaves behind him not pebbles or breadcrumbs, but drops of his own blood, sweat, and tears. He leaves them there for us to follow, through thick and thin, walking in his footsteps. Until we reach home again, safe and sound.

So we must follow his example. As the great 18th-century hymnwriter, Augustus Montague Toplady says in one of his greatest hymns, we 'tread the sacred way that Jesus watered with his blood.'

> *Let the vain world applaud or frown,*
> *still may I Heaven's path pursue:*
> *still may I stand unshook, and keep*
> *the centre of my hopes in view!*
>
> *O Light of Life, still guide my steps—*
> *without your friendly aid I stray;*
> *lead me, my God, for I am blind,*
> *direct me and point out my way.*
>
> *What is the world's good word to me,*
> *if by my God from glory driven?*
> *Can that redeem my soul from Hell,*
> *or recompense my loss of Heaven?*

Resolved to tread the sacred Way
that Jesus watered with his blood,
I bend my fixed and cheerful course
through that rough path my Master trod

The way that leads to glory lies
through ill-report, contempt and loss:
assist me to deny myself,
to follow you and bear your cross.

The way that leads to glory lies through ill-report, contempt and loss. That's the way that Jesus walked, with the cross on his shoulders, for us. And that's the way that we too must walk if we want to find our way home. There is no other way. Anyone who wants to live a godly life in Christ Jesus will face these trials.

No bright pebbles light our path to glory. The birds swoop down to eat the tasty breadcrumbs. We will not float up to heaven on a cloud of comfort, applauded and respected by the unbelieving world. Or sail into glory without a fight against our sin.

The only way home is to follow the blood.

It may not be pleasant. It will sometimes feel lonely as we place our feet in the footsteps of the one who cried 'my God, my God, why have you forsaken me?' But we know that he's been that way before, and we know where he's leading us—to an inheritance that is certain—imperishable, undefiled, and unfading, kept in heaven for us.

4

Ephesians 2:11–22

The Cross and Separation

*T*herefore *remember that at one time you Gentiles
in the flesh, called 'the uncircumcision' by what is
called the circumcision, which is made in the flesh by
hands*—[12] *remember that you were at that time separated
from Christ, alienated from the commonwealth of Israel and
strangers to the covenants of promise, having no hope and
without God in the world.*

[13] *But now in Christ Jesus you who once were far off have
been brought near by the blood of Christ.* [14] *For he himself is
our peace, who has made us both one and has broken down
in his flesh the dividing wall of hostility* [15] *by abolishing
the law of commandments expressed in ordinances, that he
might create in himself one new man in place of the two, so
making peace,* [16] *and might reconcile us both to God in one
body through the cross, thereby killing the hostility.* [17] *And
he came and preached peace to you who were far off and*

peace to those who were near. ¹⁸ For through him we both have access in one Spirit to the Father.

¹⁹ So then you are no longer strangers and aliens, but you are fellow citizens with the saints and members of the household of God, ²⁰ built on the foundation of the apostles and prophets, Christ Jesus himself being the cornerstone, ²¹ in whom the whole structure, being joined together, grows into a holy temple in the Lord. ²² In him you also are being built together into a dwelling place for God by the Spirit.

Ephesians 2:11–22.

At Christmas-time the radio starts playing all the old favourites. The feel-good songs. So we get all the classic sentimental Christmas tracks—Last Christmas, White Christmas, All I Want for Christmas, Do they know it's Christmas?

And amongst all those, for some reason we keep on hearing the John Lennon song, 'Imagine'. Because it's supposedly all about love and peace and brotherhood, and I guess the radio producers think those are obvious Christmas themes. Imagine there were no more countries, and people didn't kill each other for religion or any other reason. Everyone would live in peace, and the world would live as one.

I like the idea—a life of peace, no more war, a united world. But I'm not sure he's quite got the right prescription for it in the rest of the song. Yes, John, we *will* say you're a dreamer.

Still, the reason this is a classic is that our society retains that nagging sense of restlessness and separation—a lack of peace and unity and brotherhood—which makes us wistful for some of the things Lennon sings about.

You can see that reflected in all the Christmas messages on TV. So Her Majesty the Queen spoke a few years ago about alienation and separation in society, saying, 'Religion and culture are much in the news these days, usually as sources of difference and conflict, rather than for bringing people together.'

The Pope calls for people to come together to help create peace in the still troubled Middle East. And directly from that war-torn area, one year Channel 4 controversially asked the President of Iran to deliver an alternative to the Queen's Speech. Again, he spoke of how people are alienated from one another and how our societies are in a mess. He finished by praying for the New Year to be 'a year of happiness, prosperity, peace and brotherhood for humanity'.

Peace, unity, a brotherhood of man. That's what people seem to want, not just at Christmas, but always.

So is there a Christian answer to those universal longings of the human heart? Or are they just sentimental dreams? Does the baby in the manger have anything to offer a fractured world?

Well, the answer is contained in the passage from the Bible which is at the top of this chapter. We'll find as we look at it that it has great relevance for us in our troubled days. Because it's all about the creation of a more peaceful and united world.

It might sound like a bit of a dream. But there's nothing more certain and more solid than this. Because what we're talking about is God's plan to unite all things in heaven and earth under one head. The reason we think about these things at Christmas is that it's his birthday. God wants to bring everything under the authority and rule of Jesus. That's the big message of this letter to the Ephesians which Paul announced in chapter 1 verse 10. He announces that God has 'a plan for the fullness of time, to unite all things in [Christ], things in heaven and things on earth.'

How does he do all this? Well, according to Ephesians, God achieves this through the death of Christ on the cross. Because the longings that come to the surface at Christmas can only be fulfilled by the achievement of Christ at Easter. The longings we have at Christmas are only fulfilled on the cross.

This is one of the frequently forgotten aspects of the cross. We often speak as Christians of how Christ's death saves us from God's anger at our sin, how he takes our place and takes our punishment. How we are saved by his precious blood. But there is also a corporate dimension to what the cross achieved. Jesus didn't just come to save me personally so I can go to heaven when I die. That's glorious. But it's not the whole story.

So in this chapter, we're looking at how the cross deals with the problems of separation and hostility in our world. Ephesians 2 shows us how. The passage splits into three. So first we hear in Ephesians 2 verses 11–13 about our estrangement from God and his people. Then we hear in verses 14–18 about how Christ has reconciled enemies together to God. Then finally in verses 19–22 the conclusion is that we are no longer outsiders but an integral part of God's plan in Jesus Christ.

Before we look at how hostility has been abolished by the cross, we need to look at the problem. We need to look at how far away we were from God and from each other—the root of the problem which lies at the heart of all the mess in the world that John Lennon, the Queen, the Pope, and Mahmoud Ahmadinejad all agree we need to deal with somehow.

Remember how far away you were

So first, remember how far away you were. Let's look again at verses 11–13. Paul wants us to *remember* something:

> *remember* that at one time you Gentiles in the flesh, called 'the uncircumcision' by what is called the circumcision, which is made in the flesh by hands— *remember* that you were at that time separated from Christ, alienated from the commonwealth of Israel and strangers to the covenants of promise, having no hope and without God in the world.

So, who's he talking to? He's talking to those who are 'gentiles in the flesh', i.e. people who were not born Jews. And there's a bit of name-calling here. Such people are *called* 'uncircumcised' by the Jews; it's a term of abuse in Jewish eyes, like calling someone a barbarian or a

63

Philistine perhaps. If you are part of 'the uncircumcision' you're unclean and unacceptable.

This was one of the most fundamental divisions in the ancient world. The antagonism between Jews and Gentiles was legendary. The Jews of Jesus' day disliked outsiders. And the feeling was mutual. Gentile pagans mocked and despised the Jews, and first-century writers such as Tacitus and Juvenal commented on how with their unseen God in the clouds and their kosher food laws and Sabbaths, the Jews hated all outsiders, especially Romans, and despised their laws and ways.

If you think of Gaza, Northern Ireland in the troubles, Sunni vs. Shia in Iraq, or South Africa during apartheid, you're getting something of the flavour of the loathing and distaste that one side had for the other.

So you may have heard that in Jesus' day there literally was what verse 14 calls a 'dividing wall of hostility' in the Jewish Temple in Jerusalem, to keep Gentiles out. It had a sign over it which said something like, 'Come any closer Gentile, and you'll have only yourself to blame for your subsequent violent death.' It was not a popular Gentile tourist spot.

So the world was divided, as it is today. But there was a more fundamental problem too. Verse 12 says before God sorted us out we were godless. We were alienated from the commonwealth of Israel, strangers to the covenants of promise. We had no hope, and we didn't have God in our lives. Yes, we are separated from each other by walls of our own making. But worse than that we are separated from Christ.

Now, as Christ is just the Greek word for Messiah what he could be saying there is, you had no Messiah, no-one to save you. That would be bad enough considering what Paul has said previously in Ephesians 2 about our need to be saved from the clutches of the devil, from addiction to our own selfish appetites, and from the righteous anger of God on judgment day. We need a Messiah, a saviour, in the face of such a predicament.

But there's also another aspect to being separated from Christ. Paul has already told us in chapter 1 verse 3 that Christians have every spiritual blessing *in Christ*. It is in him, in relationship with Christ, that we have forgiveness and every other blessing.

Therefore to be separated from him means to be cut off from our only saviour and the source of every spiritual blessing. It means to be at odds with the one person who is in ultimate control of every living thing in the universe.

Have you ever felt in a group of people that you were being kept out of the loop somehow? That something important you really should know about was going on behind your back and that you weren't being let in on it? Who's next for the chop perhaps, or what's really happening behind the scenes. It feels awful doesn't it, to be out of an important inner circle? It can niggle away at you, causing suspicion, resentment, and anxiety.

Well, to be separated from Christ is to be way out of the loop, on the most important issue in the universe.

Verse 12 literally says you were separated from Christ, *having been alienated* from the commonwealth of Israel. In other words, because you were not part of Israel, God's people, that's why you were separate from Christ. You were separated from him because you were alienated from his people.

God is known in community. It isn't just about having a personal private relationship with Jesus. It is about being part of a family, a people, a society. Part of something bigger than just me.

And that's to be expected of a God who himself exists as a community of three persons in one God. God the Father, God the Son, and God the Holy Spirit have lived together and loved one another for all eternity.

And so to reflect God's character we too are called to live in community with each other, as one body. But it's not simply being part of a group that's important. What matters is that we were alienated from *God's* group. Not ethnic Israel. You don't have to be Jewish. He's talking about a spiritual reality—we need to be part of the group which inherits the promises of God and is promised a future hope. We need to be in Christ, part of Jesus' new community.

So Paul says to us in Ephesians 2, remember how far away you were. You were out of it, completely. We better appreciate what we have when we remember it wasn't always ours, and what life was like without it. We also better appreciate what we have when we realize how much it cost.

Something has changed so that peace and unity are now a possibility. Verse 13 gives us the headline: 'But now in Christ Jesus you who once were far off have been brought near by the blood of Christ.' Christ has done something to deal with the alienation, estrangement, and hopelessness of our world. He did it by shedding his blood, on the cross, for us.

But we would misunderstand this if we simply interpreted that as 'Jesus died for me so I can go to heaven.' He hasn't just taken the punishment that my sins deserve—though praise God he has done that. The rest of the passage shows us that there's even more on offer to those wise men and women who seek Jesus today.

He is our peace, says verse 14. That's not inner tranquillity—he has reconciled us, says verse 16. All of which leads us to a new state of affairs where we are no longer far off, but integrated into God's wonderful plan for the universe along with people from every nation, tribe, and type.

Christ has reconciled us

So let's look closer at what Paul says about the achievement of the cross. The first thing he says in verse 14 is that the incitement to religious hatred so characteristic of our world has been abolished. Look again at verse 14: '[Christ] himself is our peace, who has made us both one and has broken down in his flesh the dividing wall of hostility by abolishing the law of commandments and ordinances …'

Jesus has broken down the wall of hostility and hatred. That wall between Jew and Gentile has gone, the wall between those who were part of the Commonwealth of Israel, and those who were separated and alienated from that. God has made 'us both', says Paul—you gentiles as well as us Jews—we have both been made one. The religious and racial hostility between Jews and Gentiles has been abolished and peace established.

But what was it that incited such hostility in the first place? It wasn't just a literal wall built in the Jerusalem temple, any more than the wall that divides Israel from Palestine today is the real cause of the problem. No, walls are only the outworking of the underlying cause, which according to verse 15 was the law of commandments and ordinances. The Old Testament Law.

That Old Testament Law commanded Jews to keep themselves separate from the other nations. They would do this in several ways. First there were various ceremonial things which made the Jews distinctive. So by means of circumcision, food laws, and Sabbaths you could tell who was a Jew and who wasn't, who was in and who was out.

So the Old Testament law kept the peoples separate. And quite right too in many ways! God designed his Law to protect his people from sinking into immorality. It was designed to keep Gentile immorality at arm's length. That was the big message you got when it was followed. Unless you became a Jew, you should be neither trusted nor emulated. You had no chance of being accepted.

But Paul's point here is that something has changed with the arrival of Jesus Christ on the scene. His kingdom is designed to include Gentiles. The way of that Law has been abolished, because it has been fulfilled by Christ. It is now possible for Jew and Gentile to be at peace with each other, if they are both 'in Christ.'

Now, there are various wrong conclusions we can draw from that bold statement: Christ abolished the Law. Gentiles who formerly were estranged from God and separated from his people can come in. But Jesus didn't do this by lowering God's standards. He didn't just remove the wall and say, 'Everyone can now come to God, he doesn't care what you believe or how you live after that— just come to Jesus!'

Let us be clear: Jesus does not lower God's standards, as the School Examination Boards have been accused of doing in order to give out more GCSEs and A Levels.

And what Jesus did to the Law doesn't mean the first part of our Bibles are now no use, a mere historical curiosity. No, the New Testament is very clear, the God and Father of our Lord Jesus Christ *is* the God of the Old Testament. There is only one God. So the Old Testament certainly still functions as a revelation of who God is.

What Jesus has done to the Law doesn't mean that we Christians can't read the Old Testament commandments to teach us how to live as Christians. Not at all. Because Paul himself does that in this very letter. In Ephesians 6:2 he tells Ephesian Gentile Christians to obey the Fifth Commandment. And he says elsewhere that the whole

Old Testament is useful for teaching, rebuking, correcting, and training Christians in righteousness (2 Timothy 3:16). So whatever Ephesians 2 means about the abolition of the Law, it can't mean Christians should ignore the Old Testament.

But we're not looking here at the continuing use of the Law for Christians. We're rejoicing in the abolition of the Law *as a thing which keeps Jews and Gentiles separated from each other.* The Old Testament Law is not our constitution. For a time it was, and it undeniably did divide, as God designed. Now that Christ has come, though, things have changed and such separations no longer apply.

So religious hatred between Jews and Gentiles has been outlawed in Christ. Now what counts is not circumcision, food laws, and Sabbaths—but whether you know and love the Lord Jesus. And that means that peace and reconciliation are achieved. Christ has abolished the Law, so 'that he might create in himself one new man in place of the two, so making peace, and might reconcile us both to God in one body through the cross, thereby killing the hostility.'

Christ has created something new. We are part of a new humanity, a new entity. Gentiles are no longer excluded and alienated as we were in the past. So now we can be at peace with Jews without needing to become Jews with all the ceremonial and physical implications that might have.

Now, no-one needs to become a Jew in order to know God. We need to become Christians. And in fact the old Jewish way is no longer relevant. There is one *new* way to relate properly to God, it says here. So a Gentile who wants to know God and be reconciled to him must become a Christian; and a Jew who wants to know God must become a Christian. It is in Christ, as we both relate to Christ, that the hostility is taken away. Because, it says, Christ has created this new humanity 'in himself.'

So you see, in verse 15, the one new way in Christ replaces the old division. And it's also clear that Jew and Gentile are both in need of reconciliation to God. So they are both reconciled to God 'in one body', in one way, together. So there isn't a Jewish way to heaven and a Gentile way to heaven. There is one way—Christ's way, the way of the cross.

I was privileged to see a fantastic picture of this a few years ago. One Sunday evening at church we baptized, at the same service, a Jewish man and a gentile woman. A proper, kosher Jew and a radical feminist Gentile, joined together by faith in Christ and baptized in his name.

On another occasion, on a Sunday morning, I baptized a man from Communist China, a man from Buddhist Vietnam, and a woman from a Muslim family in Trinidad & Tobago. Their baptisms say to us that we are now one in Christ Jesus. Different backgrounds, races, stories. But saved and brought together in Christ. We are one.

In the summer of 2014, the 'Islamic State' in Iraq painted the Arabic letter *nun* on the doors of Christian houses and buildings, to mark them out for destruction. The governments of the West did not seem to notice this, but it touched a raw nerve for Christians around the world. Many changed their social media profile pictures to a large letter *nun*, as if to say 'We are *Nasrani*, Christians, too.' Some voluntarily painted the symbol onto their own churches and houses. Without having ever met an Iraqi Christian, perhaps, they instinctively knew that they were united with them, and in small ways like this, and in larger ways too, they demonstrated their solidarity with them, their unity in Christ.

That's what Ephesians is talking all about: God bringing everything together under Christ. The goal of this is to create peace. The cross achieves two kinds of peace—peace between different kinds of people, and reconciliation between those people and God. To reconcile us to God, Jesus must die in our place and take the punishment our sins deserve. But as he does that he doing something with us corporately too.

Bringing unity to the world through the cross

The unity created by Christ doesn't come about through force of arms, uniting people in a militaristic Caliphate. It does not happen through the forces of globalisation, uniting everyone on social media or through trade and commerce. God's plan is not like a human plan to change and conquer the world. His plan is the cross. He conquers and unites through the cross, as the vulnerable baby in the manger grows up and is crucified, in weakness.

Did you notice that emphasis throughout Ephesians 2? So we glimpse it first in verse 13 where Paul announced that 'now in Christ Jesus, you who once were far off have been brought near *by the blood of Christ.*' Then in verse 14 we learn that the abolition of the dividing wall between Jews and Gentiles was broken down *in his flesh.* And in verse 16 we hear that our reconciliation to God is achieved in one body *through the cross.*

The death of Christ in our place on the cross was the key moment in God's strategy. Because on the cross Christ did all that was necessary to bring peace and reconciliation back to this divided, fractured world and restore us to a relationship with our Father in heaven.

When he died, the righteous hostility the holy God had towards us, his selfish and unruly creatures, was also killed. He reconciled us to God through the cross, says verse 16, thereby killing that hostility. No wonder the prophet Isaiah, seeing into the future, said the Messiah would be the Wonderful Counsellor, Mighty God, the Prince of Peace.

Ultimately the gospel, the good news of Jesus, is the only hope for any fractured family or society—in Iraq, in Gaza, in Zimbabwe, in England. The gospel is the power of God to save us and also to heal our divisions, as we come together under one head, Jesus Christ. You may say that I am a dreamer. Yet I am clearly not alone.

Verse 21 tells us that we are being built together into a holy temple in the Lord. That is, in Christ, the Spirit is building us into a place for God the Father to live. The

Trinity are working together to change us and mould us into something beautiful, without spot or wrinkle or any such thing, holy and utterly without blemish. Ephesians 4 also tells us that we too should be working together—being 'eager to maintain the unity of the Spirit in the bond of peace.'

There is a unity between Christians of all types, whatever colour they are, whether male or female, middle-class or whatever. The Spirit is placing all these different bricks together to make God's temple, the Church. Christians are like LEGO bricks if you like—we're designed to fit together with other Christians, not just to stand alone.

So the application of Ephesians 2 comes right there in Ephesians 4. Are we eager to maintain the integrity of the building which God the Holy Spirit is making? That is, are we keen to ensure that there are no cracks in the brickwork, nothing that divides us or pulls us apart from one another? Because it's not like all our differences and sinful tendencies disappear overnight when we become Christians! We have to work at unity, being in practice what we truly are in Christ.

The unity of the Spirit is the unity we have with all God's chosen children because of the death of Christ. So let's not neglect what Christ did on the cross for us—like we might neglect an unwanted Christmas present we just discard and throw away. Let's not neglect this aspect of the cross, by neglecting our brothers and sisters in the church and thinking we can get by with a ruggedly individualistic faith.

Church is not a drop-in centre where we come to hear entertaining preaching, or a concert hall to enjoy excellent music. It's a construction site where blood, sweat, and tears go into fixing people and sticking them together.

Let's not do anything to break the bond of peace we have, by for instance, trying to re-erect barriers between people in the Church. We could easily fall into the trap, and do this on racial grounds. Making the black Christians in our congregation feel second rate. Patronising our Chinese brothers and sisters. Or what about introducing divisions on educational grounds: looking down on those without a degree or an A Level, or a job, as if they were not also part of Christ? Making the church just a nice place for what Bridget Jones called the 'smug marrieds', but ignoring the disciples of Jesus who are single, struggling, or sexually confused.

In him there is no Jew or Gentile, slave or free, male or female, clever or stupid, black or white, posh or pleb, rich or poor. The ground is level at the foot of the cross.

Titus 2:1–15

The Cross and Sanctification

*B*ut as for you, teach what accords with sound doctrine.
*² Older men are to be sober-minded, dignified, self-controlled, sound in faith, in love, and in steadfastness.
³ Older women likewise are to be reverent in behaviour, not slanderers or slaves to much wine. They are to teach what is good, ⁴ and so train the young women to love their husbands and children, ⁵ to be self-controlled, pure, working at home, kind, and submissive to their own husbands, that the word of God may not be reviled. ⁶ Likewise, urge the younger men to be self-controlled. ⁷ Show yourself in all respects to be a model of good works, and in your teaching show integrity, dignity, ⁸ and sound speech that cannot be condemned, so that an opponent may be put to shame, having nothing evil to say about us. ⁹ Bondservants are to be submissive to their own masters in everything; they are to be well-pleasing, not argumentative, ¹⁰ not pilfering, but showing all good faith, so that in everything they may adorn the doctrine of God our Saviour.*

¹¹ For the grace of God has appeared, bringing salvation for all people, ¹² training us to renounce ungodliness and worldly passions, and to live self-controlled, upright, and godly lives in the present age, ¹³ waiting for our blessed hope, the appearing of the glory of our great God and Saviour Jesus Christ, ¹⁴ who gave himself for us to redeem us from all lawlessness and to purify for himself a people for his own possession who are zealous for good works.

¹⁵ Declare these things; exhort and rebuke with all authority. Let no one disregard you.

Titus 2:1–15.

It's worth at this stage just re-capping on where we've got to. We looked initially at the cross and success from 1 Corinthians chapter 1. We saw how the cross undercuts all our ideas of what success looks like, as God used something weak and apparently futile to shame the strong and baffle the wise.

Then we saw in Mark chapter 10 how the cross overturns our ideas of greatness, and re-focuses our ambitions. Even the Son of Man did not come to be served, but to serve, and to give his life as a ransom for many. The cross says: greatness is serving others.

We saw how in the midst of suffering or persecution the cross gives us an example to follow, as we tread the sacred way that Jesus watered with his own blood. And we saw in the last chapter how the cross puts an end to separation.

Each time we've seen that the idea of penal substitution—that Jesus takes the punishment my sins deserve—is crucially important. We don't understand the cross without that. But we've also seen that there is more to it than *simply* that. There are depths of wisdom and knowledge for us to explore at the foot of the cross.

In this chapter we're going to explore the cross and sanctification. Now 'sanctification' is a big word, I realize, and I use it for two reasons. First, it fits into the alliteration nicely! The cross and success, the cross and service, the cross and suffering, the cross and separation, and now the cross and sanctification.

But I also use it because it's the big theological word we often use to describe the Bible's teaching on holiness, purity, living a good life. So if *justification* is how we get right with God and start the Christian life, then *sanctification* (the way we traditionally use that word) is about how we go on with Christ, how we live a godly life.

And that's what this passage in Titus 2 is all about. It's what the whole of Paul's letter to Titus is about actually. People who claim to be Christians should be godly, self-controlled men and women, living holy and upright lives.

It's no surprise to learn that the Apostle Paul relates our need to live a godly life to what Jesus has done for us. We see it there in verse 14 of Titus 2 very clearly. Look again to what he says in verse 13. We are, 'waiting for our blessed hope, the appearing of the glory of our great God and Saviour Jesus Christ, who gave himself for us to redeem us from all lawlessness and to purify for himself a people for his own possession who are zealous for good works.'

He gave himself for us to redeem us and to purify us. What we're talking about here then is the purpose of the atonement. The intention and design of the cross of Jesus Christ. What God the Father had in mind when he sent his Son to die.

Paul tells us something mind-blowing about the one who died for us. He wasn't just an innocent third party, sent to do God's dirty work and clean up after us and sort us out. He was 'our great God and Saviour Jesus Christ.'

That's not a mistake there. Paul *is* saying that Jesus is our God. There aren't many places in the New Testament where it's made *this* obvious and clear in a single verse. So let's make sure we've got this in our minds for next time someone asks us a question about the Trinity, or the Jehovah's Witnesses come knocking on the door. Titus 2:13 says Jesus Christ was not just an ordinary man. He was both man and God.

So what we have going on at the cross is God himself making atonement for us. God himself in the person of the Son, the Word made flesh, dying in our place. God giving himself up to mere human authorities, to be crucified, for the sake of mere human sinners, like us.

What we see going on at Calvary, the place where Jesus died, is of monumental significance. Father, Son, and Holy Spirit acting together in concert and perfect harmony to achieve their purpose in our salvation. And part of that salvation is our sanctification—our holiness, godliness, purity, and goodness.

As Hebrews 9 puts it, Christ 'through the eternal Spirit offered himself without blemish to God, to purify our conscience from dead works'. All three members of the Trinity working together for our salvation and sanctification.

We shouldn't forget the full identity of the one hanging there for us. It was no less than *the living God*, being put to death. The one who made us and sustains us, being snuffed out for our sake. God himself, gave himself, for us.

And what was his plan? Anybody with half a brain has a plan and a purpose before they set out to do something. It may not always be clearly defined, but every time I step out of my door I have a plan in my mind for what I want to do. So what was God, the most infinitely wise being in the universe planning to do when the Father sent the Son in the power of the Spirit?

Titus tells us three things in these verses to answer that question. And the first thing he tells us is that God gave himself up in order to purchase the lawless. He purchased the lawless.

Purchase the lawless

We see this in verse 11. 'The grace of God has appeared, bringing salvation for all people.' He came to save us, by his grace. And then verse 14—he 'gave himself up for us to redeem us from all lawlessness.'

The picture being conjured up here of course is that we need to be rescued. We need saving by our great God and *Saviour* Jesus Christ. We can't save ourselves from the predicament we're in. We need outside help to avoid a great catastrophe. And that salvation is here described using that word 'redeem'.

Christ came to redeem us, to rescue us. What from? Well, elsewhere we are said to have been redeemed from the curse of the Law. That is, we're rescued from having to face the full demands of God's holy perfect Law which we have failed to keep. Having fallen short and sinned in thought and word and deed, as we prayed earlier, we fall under his curse. We need forgiveness.

And that's what we get at the cross. In Christ, says the letter to the Ephesians, 'we have *redemption* through his blood—the forgiveness of our sins.' It's the word for paying the price to free a slave. Or the price needed to release someone from an obligation or debt.

How is that pictured here? Well, not as a debt God owes to the devil or something like that. He doesn't buy us from Satan. No, we are pictured here as being slaves to sin, to lawlessness. We're trapped into obliging and obeying our sinful and disordered desires, rather than God. The blood of Christ releases us from that debt.

That's very much in accordance with what Paul is trying to get at in his letter. He's telling Titus, one of his co-workers, what he needs to teach people in Crete, where Titus has been left after one of Paul's missionary journeys. And he says at the end of the letter, in chapter 3 verse 14, that it's important for the Christians in Crete to be good, moral, upright people. 3:14—'let our people learn to devote themselves to good works' he says.

So earlier, here in chapter 2, Paul reminds Titus that as Christians we have been purchased by God. We are no longer slaves to lawlessness and worldly passions. The kind of things that used to control us and shape our lives and ambitions—their grip on us has been loosened and destroyed by what Jesus has done on the cross for us. We now belong to God.

Purify our lives

That's what happened in the past. The grace of God appeared in Christ and brought salvation. So now, in the present, that grace also trains us. Grace saves, and grace trains. Which brings us to the second point. Jesus Christ, our great God and Saviour, gave himself for us to purchase us, and also (secondly) to purify us. He gave himself to purify us, in the here and now.

Have another look at verse 12. It says the grace of God trains us 'to renounce ungodliness and worldly passions, and to live self-controlled, upright, and godly lives in the present age.' In verse 14 it says he gave himself for us 'to redeem us from all lawlessness and to purify for himself a people for his own possession.'

So this is where the redemption of the cross kicks in to my life in the here and now. And this is what I often neglect. I think of the cross as having done something in the past. I may even think of it as having done something to secure my future. But I so often forget that it has implications in this present age.

Here also is where I can easily lapse into works and law
and guilt, of course. Having been saved by grace, we too
often burden ourselves and others with a list of do's and
don'ts, and a calendar full of events they must attend, and
a shelf full of books, as the way to walk in godliness. But
Paul—the man most famous for teaching us salvation by
grace alone—reminds us here that the very grace which
saves is the grace which also trains, and teaches us to say
no.

Grace teaches us to say no to the futile and foolish ways
in which we used to live. And it gives us new patterns of
thinking and acting instead. Like what? Well, that's why
we started with the whole of Titus chapter 2. Because the
last paragraph from verse 11 onwards is just the theology.
The first 10 verses is all the practical application. The two
are intimately related of course. Verse 11 says we should
do all the stuff in verses 1–10 *for, because, in the light of,*
verses 11–14.

So verse 1 of the chapter tells Titus to 'teach what
accords with sound doctrine', that is, teach what is healthy
for people. We use the word 'sound' in that way still, don't
we? He's 'sound in body and mind', we might say. The word
just means healthy.

We have the healthy doctrine in verses 11–14. What
accords with it, the healthy lifestyle that comes from
healthy teaching is outlined from verse 2 onwards. Titus
is told to spell it all out, because there were some people
in Crete who hadn't yet understood the link between
sound doctrine and sound living. They seemed to think,

chapter 1 says, that they could teach all sorts of weird stuff and it wouldn't matter in their lives. They professed to know God, but by their works they denied him. A veneer of religion—it sounded very spiritual perhaps. But the lifestyle didn't match, and wasn't up to scratch.

So let's look at the healthy lifestyle, for which we have been purchased by God. He bought us, he died for us, so that we would live like this. You'll notice that the way Paul talks about lifestyle he splits us into age and gender groups. So he addresses older men, older women, younger women, then younger men. He also has a word for the Christian slaves in Crete too, in their particular employment circumstances. So let's have a look at what he says to each of these groups in turn about healthy Christian living.

So older men, verse 2. Be sober-minded, dignified, self-controlled, sound in faith, in love, in steadfastness. Doesn't give us a lot of detail here, does he? But the picture conjured up is an impressive one. We know, don't we, when we've met an older man who is sober-minded, dignified, and self-controlled.

We also know when we've met an older man who is not those things. One who is instead rather immature and unstable, somewhat childish, despite his age. The kind of person you *don't* go to with a problem in your thinking or your life, because he'll be no help whatsoever.

I would hesitate to preach to older men, if it weren't for verse 15, which tells me that as a teacher in the same sort of position as Titus was, I am to exhort and rebuke you and let no-one disregard me! But are you, as an older man, all the things listed in verse 2? Granted you won't be perfect. You're a work in progress still, even if you are over 40 (that's the definition of an older man in the ancient world I think—over 40).

It gives something to aim at doesn't it? Particularly steadfastness. Are we solid, dependable, reliable, steadfast? Or do people say we're stubborn, proud, and immoveable? There may be a fine line between those things. But if we're sound in faith and sound in love we'll be good at gauging where that line is. Jesus died to push us over it.

What about older women? Verse 3. Older women likewise are to be reverent in behaviour, not slanderers or slaves to much wine. Older women who are Christians have been taught by God's grace shown to us in the cross to renounce ungodliness and worldly passions. So they shouldn't be silly or flighty. They shouldn't be gossips—that's what slanderer means here—too easy to let a good bit of gossip become a slagging off session, whatever age and gender we are!

Why does it say older women should not be 'slaves to much wine'? Odd that one. I would have expected that to apply to young men more than anything, or young binge-drinking women. Wouldn't you? But perhaps too much sherry or too much gin and tonic or too many bottles of Rosé is a temptation for older women just as much? I don't know.

But older Christian women who have been purchased by God from a lawless lifestyle need to be careful not to go back into slavery of any kind. Instead, older women are to be good examples, and to teach younger women. Teaching what is good. Teaching younger women to love their husbands and children, if they have such things. Being examples to the younger generation of what self-controlled, pure, hard-working womanhood looks like. In how they run the house, in how they behave in their marriage and in public.

All this is not just for the sake of a quiet life. But, as verse 5 says—'so that the word of God may not be reviled.' So that no-one can insult the gospel or the God whose grace saves us by pointing at the women amongst the Christians and saying '*They* don't look as if they have been redeemed and purified! They look just like any other women their age.'

Does this have anything to say to those younger women who are thinking about *work* tomorrow morning, in the cut-throat business world or a more mundane job? I think it does. Most of the young women in Crete in Titus' day would have been married with kids perhaps, struggling to know what it means to submit to their husbands, and struggling to love their children and be self-controlled with them. That's why Paul addresses them specifically, and tells them that the cross has redeemed them from a selfish life and teaches them a different way.

Yet the things he says are also applicable to those women who are not married and don't have kids, aren't they? The word self-controlled seems to come up all the time in this passage—that applies to those working in banks and offices and schools and shops too. The motivation to behave in such a way 'that the word of God may not be reviled' also applies there, doesn't it?

Verse 10 is addressed to slaves, out at work all day. So it has a certain resonance for women and men who work to earn their living. But did you see the end of verse 10? It says workers are to *adorn* the doctrine of God our Saviour. That word 'adorn' is the word from which we get our word 'cosmetics.' It has a similar meaning in Greek here, except it's about more than just make-up, lipstick and such things, but about clothing and hair-styles as well.

So the word for any women for whom the stuff about working at home and looking after your family is not so relevant, is this. When you go to work, adorn yourself in such a way that people talk about the gospel. Let your lifestyle and manner at work be such that people comment about the fact that you're a *Christian* woman, who claims to have been redeemed from a lawless way of life by a man who died on a cross for her.

Younger men. Your turn. Well, all that goes for you too when you're at work. But look at verse 6 as well. Be self-controlled. Be a model of good works. And you're meant to do that in such a way that those who oppose Christianity will feel ashamed about the silly things they say about it. Because everyone who knows younger Christian men *knows* that they are decent, honest, honourable guys who are a pleasure to be around and to work with. That's how it should be.

Paul then addresses Titus directly, who was probably therefore a younger man himself. What he says applies to all of us in a way, because we're all meant to be talking to others about Jesus, and teaching them about what he's done to save us and to train us. And to be doing that with integrity, dignity, and healthy words. 'Show yourself in all respects to be a model of good works, and in your teaching show integrity, dignity, and sound speech that cannot be condemned, so that an opponent may be put to shame, having nothing evil to say about us.'

All this could sound a bit obvious. A bit bourgeois perhaps. A bit homely and simple. Hardly revolutionary. But try putting it into practice out there, in an environment which is controlled by worldly passions and ungodly ambitions. Then it's not so easy to be in practice what the gospel says we are—purchased by God, purified for him.

These are the things which the cross was designed to achieve. It saves us from a life of going with the flow of the world. Jesus died to save us, but he also died to make us different. That was the plan. So if we're not different, then we've missed something in our doctrine, and are not adorning the gospel in the eyes of the world—however good we are at talking about it.

Possess his elect

Finally, it was also God's plan to purify for himself a people for his own possession, as verse 14 puts it. Jesus died to purchase the lawless, to purify our lives, and finally to possess his elect.

I put it that way because that's how Paul speaks of God's people at the start of this letter. He says in chapter 1 that he was appointed an apostle 'for the sake of the faith of *God's elect* and their knowledge of the truth which accords with godliness.'

So in chapter 2 verse 14 when we're told that the purpose of the cross was in order to purify for himself a people—the people he's talking about are his elect, special, chosen people. The word used in 2:14 for 'his own possession' is the word used in the Greek Old Testament in Exodus 19, where God describes Israel as his *treasured* possession.

Jesus died for his treasured possession. As an old hymn puts it, of Christ and his church, 'From heaven he came and sought her, to be his holy bride, with his own life he bought her, and for her life he died.'[1]

We are the crown jewels as far as he is concerned, and nothing was too much to get his hands on us. We were given to him by the Father. So he gave himself up for us, to redeem us, and to purify us. We are the object of his affection, and always have been. He had us in mind from the word go. It was always his plan to save us and make us the kind of people who are zealous for good works (verse 14).

He loved us from before the foundation of the world. He is eternal: he will never stop loving us, because he never began. He gave himself up for us to save us and redeem us. He's given us his word, the word of the apostles, for the sake of our faith and our knowledge of the truth.

That truth has now been revealed to all the world, and published far and wide as verse 11 says, for the salvation of all. What Jesus did on the cross is sufficient for all who come to him.

And one day he will come back, to take possession of us for good, on that great and glorious day. We're not as shiny and as sparkling now as we will be then. But verse 13 says we are waiting 'for our blessed hope, the appearing of the glory of our great God and Saviour Jesus Christ.' What a glorious day it will be. He is coming back to get us, to possess his elect, for whom he died.

So in the light of what he's done on the cross, and in light of that glory that's to come, what shall we do while we wait?

Finish then, your new creation, Lord Jesus. Pure and spotless let us be, while we wait for your coming in glory. Take away the love of sinning, change us from within until that great and glorious day when we stand before you—those you have ransomed from out of every tribe and language and people and nation. Make us as pure now as we will be then, for your greater glory, and the adornment of your gospel, that others might be drawn to you, our great God and Saviour. Amen.

Colossians 2:6–23

The Cross and Supremacy

In our final chapter, let's look at the victory of the cross, how on the cross Christ triumphs over all his enemies.

The Supreme King

Jesus is the supreme king of the universe. But this is a hidden theme, in the Gospels. It doesn't look as if Jesus is the supreme king, as he's led to his death by a pack of political plotters and jealous religious conspirators. He looks anything but strong and mighty and victorious.

In Matthew's Gospel, the writer paints a picture for us which is full of irony and subtlety, if only we have eyes to see it. So in Matthew 27 verse 27 we see King Jesus with a whole battalion of soldiers, an Imperial Guard, inside a Palace. He is clothed in a scarlet or purple robe—the sign of kingship and imperial dignity.

In his hand they place a sceptre as a symbol of his authority. And on his head they place a crown. Then the whole battalion kneels before him, saying 'Hail, King of the Jews'.

This is what Jesus deserves. He deserves a coronation, and to be given all the dignity and honour and glory and power of kingship. The man who served others, who healed the sick, the blind, the lame, who walked on water, fed the hungry, and compelled the wind and waves to obey his voice. He deserves to be hailed as his people's king— and king of the world, which he made and sustains.

But that's not *quite* the picture is it? The Palace is not his own. It's a court, where he has been unjustly condemned to die. It's a prison, really, from which he is being led out to die.

The soldiers are not his respectful bodyguards. They are there to mock him and beat him and spit on him and prevent him getting away. His crown is made not of fine gold and sparkling jewels, but of sharp spiky thorns which cruelly cut in to his bloodstained brow with every movement of his whipped and tired body.

The sceptre of his rule ... a reed, a bit of straw blown about by the wind. Wilting and drooping in his hands as a symbol of the authority they thought he had, just as his head was bowed down and limp upon his shoulders.

It's quite a scene isn't it? The King of Kings and Lord of Lords beaten and made fun of and then led like a lamb to the slaughter. And over his head on the cross, it says in

Matthew 27:37, they put a sign saying 'This is Jesus, the King of the Jews.'

They certainly didn't mean it. But this *was* his coronation. The cross to which they nailed him *was* his throne. You turn over just a page in the Gospel and that same man, once covered in blood and sweat and spit, is rightly covered in glory. Because of what he does on that cross, he can say, 'All authority in heaven and on earth has been given to me' (Matthew 28:18).

As it was prophesied in the Garden of Eden, the devil finally managed to bruise Christ's heel, with the nails that pierced him and pinned him to the wood. But this Pyrrhic victory of evil over good, in this cruel and callous death, was destined to be the very thing which enabled Christ to crush the serpent's head forever.

He *is* the supreme king. The king of the universe. And he was crowned by that rowdy bunch of Roman soldiers, and hoisted up on to his throne with arms outstretched to the world, his dominion, with nails in his hands and his feet. They didn't know what they were doing. But they crowned the Lord of Glory.

Perhaps they were just following orders. His enemies certainly thought this was the end of him. How they must have laughed and rubbed their hands together with glee as they contemplated his demise. The devil thought this was his finest hour. God's very own Son surrounded and cut off and done for.

But the reason the Son of God appeared was to destroy the works of the evil one. He came to conquer death and to steal the keys of Hell right out of the devil's hand at the very moment when it seemed that all was lost. He got right up close, and it appeared that Satan had beaten him and secured the victory. Then Jesus snatched it all away, the very second he died.

As the Psalms say, the kings of the earth set themselves, and the rulers were gathered together, against the Lord and against his Anointed One. And what did they achieve? Only the very things which God had predestined and planned to happen (Acts 4:27–28). In the death of Christ, God subverted the mighty of this world and the powers and authorities in the heavenly realms. They meant to harm his Son. But he planned it for good.

But how did he bring good out of this? How did a moment of apparent disaster and defeat become the moment which Christians refer to as 'Good Friday'? It looked anything but good. Part of the answer is found in the following passage from Paul's letter to the Colossians. What we see ironically hidden in the Gospels, here has its clearest exposition.

Therefore, as you received Christ Jesus the Lord, so walk in him, ⁷ rooted and built up in him and established in the faith, just as you were taught, abounding in thanksgiving.

⁸ See to it that no one takes you captive by philosophy and empty deceit, according to human tradition, according to the elemental spirits of the world, and not according to Christ. ⁹ For in him the whole fullness of deity dwells bodily, ¹⁰ and you have been filled in him, who is the head of all rule and authority. ¹¹ In him also you were circumcised with a circumcision made without hands, by putting off the body of the flesh, by the circumcision of Christ, [12] having been buried with him in baptism, in which you were also raised with him through faith in the powerful working of God, who raised him from the dead. [13] And you, who were dead in your trespasses and the uncircumcision of your flesh, God made alive together with him, having forgiven us all our trespasses, [14] by cancelling the record of debt that stood against us with its legal demands. This he set aside, nailing it to the cross. [15] He disarmed the rulers and authorities and put them to open shame, by triumphing over them in him.

[16] Therefore let no one pass judgment on you in questions of food and drink, or with regard to a festival or a new moon or a Sabbath. [17] These are a shadow of the things to come, but the substance belongs to Christ. [18] Let no one disqualify you, insisting on asceticism and worship of angels, going on in detail about visions, puffed up without reason by his sensuous mind, [19] and not holding fast to the Head, from whom the whole body, nourished and knit together through its joints and ligaments, grows with a growth that is from God.

[20] If with Christ you died to the elemental spirits of the world, why, as if you were still alive in the world, do you submit to regulations—[21] 'Do not handle, Do not taste, Do not touch'[22] (referring to things that all perish as they are used)—according to human precepts and teachings? [23] These have indeed an appearance of wisdom in promoting self-made religion and asceticism and severity to the body, but they are of no value in stopping the indulgence of the flesh.

Colossians 2:6–23.

Did you catch that in verse 15? 'God disarmed the rulers and authorities and put them to open shame, by triumphing over them in him'. In Christ. Or as it could be translated, 'by it', that is, by the cross.

This crystallises the whole theme of the death of Christ as a victory. And it's part of Paul's teaching in this letter to enable the Christians in Colossae to stand firm in a hostile environment. To stand firm as believers when the world is against them; and to stand firm against those within the church itself who were leading them astray.

The Strong Knot

Basically Paul says we were so tied to Christ, so united to him, that when he died, he took us with him. A *strong knot* binds the Lord Jesus to his people. So that whatever is true of him, is true of us if we are 'in him', if we believe and trust and cling to him.

Let's look at what he says about this union we have with Christ in a bit more detail. Paul says 'in Christ the whole fullness of deity dwells bodily, and you have been filled in him, who is the head of all rule and authority.' So he's saying that Jesus Christ is God incarnate. He is full of God, and can't be 'more God' than he is.

And 'in him' we have been filled too. Not so that we are God, of course. But so that we are as full of God and as one with God as it is possible for mortal human beings to be. He is the head, we are the body, as it were. His supremacy over all rule and authority is for our benefit.

If we're 'in him', if we're Christians, then we're full. We've got it all.

It doesn't say we 'can be full' if we follow a certain regime. It doesn't say we 'will be full' if we persevere and try hard enough. It doesn't say we 'can fill ourselves' by doing certain things. No. We 'have been filled', if we are in him.

According to verse 11, we have also been circumcised! In him, that is, in Christ, united to him. Not literally circumcised—that would be rather painful and unnecessary. But spiritually speaking, because spiritually, circumcision was about putting off the flesh, dying. And if we are tied to Christ then when he died, when he put off his flesh, we died too.

This is also symbolised in baptism, says Paul. The water goes over us, we symbolically die and are buried with Christ in baptism. We're also raised again, just as Jesus was. The link here is always 'what God did for Jesus, he has also done for Christians.' We're tied to him, like a body attached to a head.

So we were 'raised with him through faith in the powerful working of God, who raised Jesus from the dead.' Faith in God's power to raise the dead is all we need to be made alive.

Then in verse 13 he begins to talk about forgiveness. And verse 14 speaks of the cancelling of the record of debt that stood against us with its legal demands. Now, we certainly have a picture of that in the recent financial crisis don't we? Huge debts have been racked up—by individuals with mortgages and loans, by banks who have lent money without adequate security, by governments who have rescued the banks. We now have a huge national debt running into billions.

Well just imagine that every time you sin, every time you think a thought or say a word or do something which makes God unhappy you incur a debt of £10. If we only sin once a day, then by the time we die our debt to God will be about £250,000.

But what if we cross the line more than once a day? Or fail to do something which God has said we should? Twice a day would seem too conservative an estimate wouldn't it? Once an hour perhaps? Maybe more. Then my life's debt will easily reach a few million pounds. I don't need to be an accountant to know it will be way beyond my ability to pay.

And the truth is, to ignore the Creator of the Universe for even a second, to rebel against his goodness and to fall short of his commands *even once*, is treason really. Much more serious than a tenner. So our debt is incalculable. And we can't just print more money and pay it off that way ('quantitative easing' as economists call it). Try a few good works and hope they'll stack up enough credit. Spiritual 'quantitative easing' won't work.

Every time you see a big number in the news—a billion pounds, a trillion dollars, remember … I owe God much more than that.

But the situation is more serious than the powerful people in the world can deal with. The G20, the IMF, the United Nations, and the World Bank cannot solve our spiritual crisis. But Jesus did. He took the record of our debt and nailed it to the cross. The very thing which Satan uses against us—our sin and guilt and inability to do what is right—Jesus took it with him when he died.

So the rulers and authorities, that is, demonic powers, the hordes of hell, the devil's minions, have nothing to say against us now. It's all gone. Done and dusted, for those who are attached to the head, Jesus Christ.

So if Satan tempts me to despair, and tells me of my guilt within, upwards I look and see him there, who made an end to all my sin. I look to Jesus who died on the cross to disarm my enemies.

He took away the mud that the devil tries to sling at me. 'You're not good enough for God' he says. 'You sin too much to be a real Christian'. 'How could God love someone who's done *that* and *that* and *that*' he snarls, pointing at all the things I'm most ashamed of. 'Call yourself a Christian' he whispers, 'I don't know why you bother even trying—you keep making a mess of it, you hypocrite.'

Every time he says that, I need to remember my debt was paid at the cross. Yes, on my own I am spiritually bankrupt. But all of that debt has been written off. I owe nothing anymore. Jesus paid it all. If I'm part of 'Jesus Incorporated', then I have a clean slate—and a balance sheet in profit even.

So this passage says I am as full as I can be in Christ. I'm marked out by the things that have happened to me *in him*. I'm alive in the one who was raised from death, and triumphant in the one who shamed the strong and defeated the devil on the cross. I'm forgiven.

Because of what Jesus did with my debt and sin, because he was punished in my place, he has beaten the devil, who has no hold or claim on me anymore. It's important to notice, of course, that if I am still liable for the debt, if I am still liable for divine punishment, then Jesus hasn't won at all. Christ can only be the victor if he is first my penal substitute.

The Subtle Kidnap

But why does Paul stress these things here? Well, the answer is in his application. The answer is in verse 8. See to it, he says, that no-one takes you captive. And further down in verse 16 'let no-one pass judgment on you'. And in verse 18 'let no-one disqualify you.' He's worried about Christians being kidnapped, taken captive, excluded, and disqualified.

I think these are all different ways of saying 'watch out, there's danger about.' What kind of danger? Well, a very subtle one, that can attack us from several angles. What does Paul say about it?

First, he says in verse 8 that our kidnappers are philosophy and empty deceit based on human traditions and 'the elemental spirits of the world'. In short, alternative philosophies and understandings of life and spirituality, which are not anchored in Christ and properly related to him.

Now, some people have taken that as a command to avoid anything which sounds philosophical or logical.

They run a mile from *any* kind of tradition, especially theological traditions, that is ways in which people have talked about God in the past.

Such a wholesale rejection of any systematic or historical awareness can't be what Paul's getting at of course. Because Paul's own method of preaching and teaching, the apostolic pattern for guarding and protecting people from error is to teach *doctrine*: careful, reasoned, systematic teaching based on the tradition handed down to him from Christ.

So Paul interweaves a whole bunch of themes in verses 8–15, including the concept of fullness, the deity of Christ, circumcision, baptism, resurrection, forgiveness, atonement, and demonic forces. His point is that unless we relate these things *properly* we will be carried off by false teaching. We'll be led into all kinds of strange and eccentric practices which have the appearance of wisdom from a human perspective but ultimately are of no value.

Other people were forgetting these basic truths and over-emphasising secondary matters perhaps. So Paul shows us how to relate them all to Christ in what looks very much like a piece of finely crafted systematic theology—that is, carefully worked out and thought-through doctrine.

It's interesting to note that he doesn't just point them to a single verse in the Bible to prove his point. He properly handles the whole Bible and relates Scripture to Scripture in the correct way to paint a much more persuasive and coherent picture of our salvation and security in Christ.

We all have a big-picture framework in the back of our minds. What Paul does here is encourage us to make sure we are developing that in a way that is self-aware, deliberate, and rigorously Christ-centred. That's the lesson for us here in how to think and reason as a Christian. It's Paul's application to our method of doing theology, if you like.

If we don't think carefully about doctrine, or are not able to reason things through clearly and make proper deductions from the things God has revealed, then we are in danger. We're in danger from those who can make plausible arguments in their expositions of the Bible.

That's what I think the false teachers were doing in Colossae. So let's look at the other dangers in this passage which Paul mentions. He says in verse 16 that we are not to allow people to judge us. Particularly in questions of food and drink and special religious days.

How were they doing that? I don't think it takes a huge leap of imagination to see that if a preacher at Colossae was doing a series of sermons on the Old Testament, say, it would be easy for him to point to the food laws or the Sabbath regulations there and say, 'Hey, look, these are biblical things to do. So we should be doing them too if we want to please God.'

What's wrong with that logic? Nothing in a way. Except that it entirely ignores Christ! It neglects to mention that in Christ we now have the substance, and these food laws and religious festivals are merely the shadows and models to help us understand him. They are the dots for us to join, the rough pencil sketches—whereas in Christ we have the full colour, multi-layered, 3-dimensional reality.

So if someone is playing in the shadows, it would be kind to try and correct them, and bring them out into the full light of day. But you certainly don't want to let *them* tell you what sunshine is. Maybe we can't stop people literally passing judgment on us, being judgmental, but we should make sure that what they think doesn't faze us or deflect us from the truth which is in Christ.

How do we as a church or as individuals 'pass judgment' on people in regard to their religious observances, as Colossians puts it? In previous generations, some would insist that Christians should not drink, smoke, or go to the cinema. This may sound strange to us now, but do we have our own taboos which are equally unbiblical?

There is a fine line on some issues—it is of course wrong for Christians to get drunk (Ephesians 5:18) so some things about what we drink, for instance, are right to be clear on. But must Christians always have a quiet time, attend a small group, educate their kids a particular way, read a particular newspaper, serve on a summer camp, wear pink pyjamas or whatever the latest thing is, in order to be accepted by us?

Are we so insecure in Christ, that we think we must do these things to be accepted by him and by others? Because we don't need to be. We are accepted by faith alone in Christ alone. That's related to the third danger here which is that people may try to disqualify us, verse 18.

To be 'disqualified' is sporting imagery. Lewis Hamilton would understand it, and so would any jockeys in the Grand National who try to go around the fences rather than jumping them. Religious people do sometimes like to set themselves up as referees, so they get to decide who is in and who is out. But as Colossians chapter 1 says, God the Father has qualified us (if we're Christians) to share in his inheritance. So no-one else has the right to pronounce us off-side.

It seems people in Colossae were insisting on asceticism—rigorous self-denial—and 'worship of angels' which probably means some kind of angelic style of worship rather than actually bowing down to angels. They felt that if you were truly 'in' you'd do the things they did, and have the experiences they had—in this case visions, angelic spiritual worship (a robed choir? A charismatic worship band?), and not touching or eating certain things.

But that's all a load of rubbish, says Paul. What matters is not all that but our relationship to the head, verse 19, our relationship to Jesus. So if there are cliques and supposedly elite circles within our churches—within your church—that you feel you can never be a part of unless you … whatever it is … then don't let that bother you. Don't hanker after acceptance by that group. What matters is how you are related and relating to Christ.

So the question which bothers us when we arrive at church on Sunday should not be 'how can I get myself into that particular set, or that gang.' But am I 'in Christ' by faith? *Because if I'm in him, then it doesn't matter whether I am 'in' anywhere else.*

If I'm in Christ, I cannot be disqualified for the greatest prize in the universe. So we mustn't allow anything or anyone to kidnap us, to drag us away from Christ. Or to judge us and make us feel second class or disqualified. However plausible they might sound, whatever their credentials as 'great leaders', however impressive their spiritual CV.

We must remain rooted and grounded in Christ and walk in him as best we know how from our study of his word. Let no-one deflect us with human wisdom and worldly criteria for judging spiritual success. Let no-one throw us off-course with a demand for more than we already have in Christ before they will accept us.

That kind of 'who cares?' attitude, of course, is what got Jesus crucified. His failure to keep merely human traditions is what angered the influential movers and shakers in the church of his day. Because he was so radically focused on pleasing God alone, he didn't pander to those who proudly thought they were the cream of the crop, and had the inside track. For his refusal to walk in their ways, they built up a case, a charge sheet against him, and used it to literally nail him.

So what we learn from all this, is that defeat or obscurity in the eyes of the powerful is utterly unimportant. Only the eyes of faith can perceive where true victory lies. The faith which alone unites us to Christ, and the faith which gives us (as Ephesians chapter 1 says) every spiritual blessing in the heavenly realms *in him*. The faith which says Christ alone is my king—and it's his approval alone that I will seek.

As I said at the start, this is in some measure a secret and hidden wisdom. None of the demonic forces which struggle against God and his people understand it. If they did, they would not have crucified the Lord of Glory. Because in his very weakness we find strength. In his alienation, we are reconciled to God. In his rejection, we have our acceptance. In his death, there is victory and life.

That's the poetry of the gospel, and the multifaceted beauty of the cross of our Lord Jesus Christ.

Endnotes

Preface: The Heart of the Cross

1 'Hallelujah! What a Saviour!' by Philip Bliss (1875).

2 I have explored some of the reasons for this in Lee Gatiss (ed.), *Confident and Equipped: Facing Today's Challenges in the Church of England* (London: Lost Coin Books, 2014), 20–21.

3 Leon Morris, *The Apostolic Preaching of the Cross* (Grand Rapids: Eerdmans, 1994), 209.

4 Ibid. 213.

5 From the song, 'In Christ Alone' by Keith Getty and Stuart Townend. Copyright © 2001 Kingsway Thankyou Music.

6 John Stott, *The Cross of Christ* (Leicester: IVP, 1989), 159.

7 Garry Williams in David Peterson (ed.), *Where Wrath and Mercy Meet: Proclaiming the Atonement Today* (Carlisle: Paternoster, 2001), 97–98.

8 J. I. Packer, 'What Did the Cross Achieve?' in *Celebrating the Saving Work of God: Collected Shorter Writings of J. I. Packer* (Carlisle: Paternoster, 1998), 121.

9 Jeffery, Ovey, Sach, *Pierced for Our Transgressions: Rediscovering the Glory of Penal Substitution* (Nottingham: IVP, 2007), 203.

Chapter 2: The Cross and Service

1 Derek Tidball, *The Message of Leviticus* (Leicester: IVP, 2005), 284.

Chapter 5: The Cross and Sanctification

1 'The Church's One Foundation' by Samuel Stone.